Broken

Into

Brilliance

Volume 1

A collection of stories from beautiful, brilliant, courageous, and determined women

Book Compilation Visionary and Publisher

Tanicia "Shamay Speaks" Currie

Mother~Author~Publisher~Event Planner/Host~Entrepreneur

925-421-0221

Shamayspeaks@gmail.com

www.WriteItAwayPublishing.com

Published by Write It Away Publishing & Shamay Speaks
www.WriteItAwayPublishing.com

Book cover designed by Shauny B with KnockSmith Productions www.knocksmithmagazine.com

Editing Services Provided by: **Dayna Plummer**

Printed in the United States of America

ISBN: 978-0-9966729-3-1

Let Write It Away Publishing help you become a published author!

Www.WriteItAwayPublishing.Com

Contact Shamay today for more information and publishing packages!

925-421-0221

ShamaySpeaks@gmail.com

Dedication:

I dedicate this book to all the women who have stepped out of their comfort zone and taken a chance by following their dreams of becoming a published author by sharing their stories. I also dedicate this book to the single mothers out there who never give up on their goals. I thank all the women who believed in me to lead them during their journey to authorship. I truly appreciate every courageous woman that has allowed me to coach and assist them in accomplishing their goals. Lastly, I dedicate this to my daughter, Laniyah. Laniyah, mommy is going to leave an amazing legacy for you and show you that you can do anything you set your mind to. I love you baby girl; you are my BEST BLESSING and Godsend!

Synopsis:

Broken Into Brilliance is a collection of short stories from powerful, brilliant, courageous, and determined women who are ready to spread their message by sharing their stories. This book features amazing women from different walks of life who have gained strength and wisdom from their past while learning to move forward. The book's visionary, Tanicia "Shamay Speaks" Currie, believes that God has the power to show us that during times when you may have felt broken, there's beauty in coming out of that broken place and overcoming those broken feelings. Being able to break through the rough times or circumstances in life is what plays a role in your brilliance as you step out into your purpose. We all have a story that can provide someone with insight, inspiration, and motivation. Being a five time author herself, Tanicia believes that sharing your story can be the first step to healing and overcoming your past experiences, as she feels her first published book served as her therapy process. Always have faith in knowing that you can still be brilliant and resilient despite the cards life has dealt you. Be encouraged!

Table of Contents

Foreword

It is a blessing and an honor to have been asked to write the foreword, as my experience with Tanicia has helped me get out of my comfort zone and strive to do better each day. When I first met Tanicia it was in the summer of 2015 at her first book signing. The book that I had been waiting for was *"Deep Within I Knew He Wasn't For Me."* Prior to her book signing I had seen flyers about the event. I was very excited that someone had written a book dealing with red flags in a relationship. I told myself that I would make sure I had no plans that day so I could be there. I was determined to be there early and that was when I met Tanicia for the first time. She was very humbled and came up to me to shake my hand to welcome me to her book signing. I remember telling myself that I had always wanted to tell my story in a book just like she had done. As she did the Q&A she asked the people in the room if they had any comments. When some of the people gave feedback she caught me off guard by pointing to me to see if I had anything to say. With tears in her eyes, as I could see she was surrounded by people who had come out to support her and give positive feedback, I thanked her for bringing awareness to the community about a topic that some people try to keep silent. I also I told her about my two daughters. After the event she signed my book and I decided to continue to follow her on social media as I would plan to attend any other events she may have. Around November of that same year I saw her again at the store as she was preparing to get things ready for the women's brunch. The connection was made at the brunch as she encouraged me to ask a business question and also she introduced me to someone who has helped her. I realized that Tanicia genuinely cared about others. With her determination to help other women share their story, she gave me and the other women the opportunity to become authors. My first book will be coming out in November. One thing about Tanicia is that she has taught me to help someone else succeed and that you are not alone in your journey. She also understands what it means to be broken and to put the pieces back together in your life so that you can live out your purpose and do what God has called you to do. There are people who are waiting for you to share your story so that you can be an encouragement to them and let them know that with God all things are possible. You will be blessed by this book as the authors share their stories about the things that they had to overcome and how they are stepping into their purpose. Instead of playing the victim they tapped into their brilliance in spite of their brokenness, and they relearned themselves and discovered the hidden talents that were inside of them. They are choosing to live a victorious life of strength and courage. Broken Into Brilliance will give you hope that no matter what you been through there is a genius inside of you ready to come out, like a caterpillar in a cocoon that is waiting to turn into a butterfly.

Keisha Frowner

Keisha Frowner

Author ~ Educator ~ Speaker ~ Mother

http://keishafrowner.wixsite.com/author

Email:klaugh983@yahoo.com

Phone: (925)238-8859

Broken

to

Brilliant

"Open Wounds"

By

Book Compilation Visionary and Publisher

Tanicia "Shamay Speaks" Currie

Mother~Author~Publisher~Event Planner/Host~Entrepreneur

925-421-0221

Shamayspeaks@gmail.com

www.ShamaySpeaks.com

www.WriteItAwayPublishing.com

<u>What Is An Open Wound?</u>

An open wound. Hmmm what is an open wound? You know, like that first cut you got that made you cry your eyes out and you wanted mommy to kiss it and give you a Band-Aid? Once mommy kissed it, everything was all better. An open wound can be an open sore/injury where medicine is needed to properly heal the wound, right? Those wounds are normal, but we may have internal wounds from our life experiences, our choices, our upbringing/childhood, our past, and much more. A Band-Aid, according to Dictionary.com, is "a makeshift, limited, or temporary aid or solution that does not satisfy the basic or long-range need (noun)." You know with normal wounds/cuts, you can apply some ointment and heal within a week or so; however, the open wounds am I talking about require more than just some ointment and a Band-Aid. Some may even require professional counseling. If you apply a Band-Aid to the open wounds I am speaking about, that Band-Aid will eventually fall off and the wound can open again. Sometimes with these open wounds, we tend to simply keep replacing the Band-Aid each time it falls off. We may feel as if the wound is healed each time we apply a new Band-Aid but unfortunately that's not the case for most of us. These open wounds affect us internally, which is why that "Band-Aid" I am speaking of can never usually fully heal that open wound. The Band-Aid that I am speaking about can be considered what some of us call "sweeping it under the carpet," leading us to think that not dealing with an issue is a way to deal; however, in reality you may just be prolonging the consequences of not dealing with the issue (i.e. the open wound). Life would be so much easier if we could just put a Band-Aid on all of our problems and our past hurts and then forget about them, right? Unfortunately, we can't bandage and forget about things that have lasting effects on us such as our dysfunctional upbringing, past abuse, having an absent parent, and much more. If only a Band-Aid could really fix these types of open internal wounds. Keep in mind that when I speak of an open wound, everything is based on your perception of your particular situation or background.

How Some of Us Deal With Our Open Wounds

Some of us choose to heal these open wounds in a variety of ways, and some of us are fortunate enough to be able to just move past it; however, for a large majority of us it's not that simple at all. Many people choose to self-medicate their emotions to deal with their open wounds. Some turn to drugs while others may ignore them until a situation in life re-opens them. For example, drug and alcohol addiction is a very common way through which many people choose to deal with/ heal their open wounds: *"Psychological causes of drug addiction. ... Sexual or physical abuse, neglect, or chaos in the home can all lead to psychological stress, which people attempt to 'self-medicate' (decrease the stress's pain through drug use). This self-medication becomes a cause of drug addiction."* ** On the other hand, there are those that unfortunately were raised in a home where drug addiction was present when they were children; therefore, many of our parents were not fully present because their addiction superseded parental priority. Drug addiction is not the only addiction we may have. Some of us have addictions to food, shopping, and even repeatedly staying in unhealthy and toxic relationships and more.

There are some of us who have open wounds from past hurts such as sexual and/or emotional abuse, and these are some of the toughest wounds to heal. Some of us begin to have issues with learning to love ourselves because the abuse cuts so deep. From not knowing how to effectively love yourself, you may create a habit of entering toxic and/or unhealthy relationships. Unfortunately, some of us attempt to heal these wounds by jumping from relationship to relationship; rationalizing why one is less toxic than the last. Sometimes, we may try to fill a void that we have but don't know how to deal with in the right way. There are many wounds that come from many different circumstances that have occurred in our lives, but it's all a matter of how we choose to deal with them.

What's Required When Dealing With Open Wounds

In my experience dealing with my own open wounds, I have thought a lot about how I would heal and move forward without constantly revisiting that wound. I want to speak about my wounds in hopes that I can reach someone going through something similar, though they may not even realize that their wounds are still open. One of the first things I did while I was in college was take advantage of the free counseling they provided at the student health center. It's been my experience that many of us within the black community feel like counselling is not necessary, which to me is the furthest from the truth. Many of us think someone has to be "crazy" to need counselling. You may have people in your family or even friends make comments like, "You are a grown woman now so just get over it." We all know that it's much easier said than done and we also know others can't know what we experience unless they have walked in our shoes. I have been to counselling three different times in the last 16 years and each time it really helped me. With that being said, please don't allow others' opinions or fear talk you out of getting help. Counselling can help you cope and slowly work through internal issues from your past, and it helps you get to the root of your problem(s). Many of us want to deal with the problem but not the root of the problem. Think of a tree: you can cut down a tree but the root will remain. This is the same for our open wounds: we can medicate and Band-Aid them but most of the time, the wound remains. If the tree's roots then it can grow back again, just like your wound.

Coping With Open Wounds

There are certain requirements that must take place or be in place when you are dealing with open wounds in order to cope with them throughout life. I want to be super real and to the point: we have to be able to identify and check those emotions stemming from those open wounds to be mindful and correct the behavior. Yup, we must "check ourselves!" Check our thoughts, feelings, and emotions to move forward day after day because the wounds are still open. You can't correct what you don't realize. You must BE in and STAY in a place of constant intentional growth and shifting of your life and mindset. You must be aware of the times that you slip back into the old you; you must also accept the old you, check the old you, and be accountable for the new you. "Therefore, if anyone is in Christ, the new creation has come: The old has gone, the new is here!" (2 Corinthians 5:17 NIV) You must understand that there will be times where you will feed the old you and feel down. There will be times that you will feel like you cannot continue to change, but stay in prayer. What you must remember is that you cannot and must not linger in those places of doubt and fear, for long if you do, the devil will attack you. Remember, the devil preys on your weaknesses, and that doesn't mean that we can never be weak because we all have weak moments. What that means is that you cannot linger in those weak moments because it can lead to depression. Lingering and depression allow the devil to attack you, so you must build up your strong suit of healthy consistent emotional armor. It's like a knight that puts on his armor; you must wear your armor at all times. Another requirement of coping with open wounds is self-discipline, and disciplining yourself and knowing when you're reverting back to the ways that you did not like before. We all have periods of regression, but you choose how long you stay in that period.

This does not mean that you will never revert back or have momentary times where you revert back to who you don't want to be. Know that God has a way of changing and shifting your life for the better, and you gotta trust Him. Again, none of this means that you will have a perfect life and never have to visit those old places; however, the good news is the more you build that armor, the better off you'll be when coping with the times that you visit those old places. You must be intentional about your change, your personal and spiritual growth.

It's important to evaluate who you have around you that can contribute to the consistency of improving yourself. This means trying your best to stay around like-minded people who want to see you grow. You are required to take inventory of everything that's working in your life and what's not working in your life so that you are able to know what is a priority and what needs to be removed.

It's a requirement for you to have faith and to trust God in the midst of the storm as well as in the midst of the good times. Don't only trust God when you're in the storm, trust Him when he's pulling you through the storm and when you're out of the storm. Regardless of if the storm lasts four months or four years, He'll pull you through. There will be times and you will have moments where you have to check yourself! Remember that song, "Check yourself before you wreck yourself" by Ice Cube? There is absolutely nothing wrong with checking yourself and telling yourself to get it together! I check myself all the time because I used to not have a lot of healthy self-control. I don't have total control, but I am intentionally and consistently working at it. I don't just work at it on Monday and Wednesday and Fridays, I work at it at all times. This is a never-ending process, but the beauty is the more intentional and consistent you become, the easier it will be. Consistency is KEY!

Get Serious About Moving Past Those Open Wounds; You're Going to Feel Like a NEW You!

Part of coping is forgiveness. You can't change or control anyone but YOU! Like they say, forgiveness is for YOU, not those who wronged you, even if they are the root of your open wound. Part of releasing the old you is forgiving others as well as forgiving yourself. Don't become that bitter wounded person, because like they say, "hurt people, hurt people!" I was at church this past weekend and the pastor preached a great message about letting go of bitterness towards those who have wronged you. Pastor Nepstad said, "Bring their balance to ZERO." This means that you no longer hold unto the expectation that the person owes you something. "14 -For if you forgive other people when they sin against you, your heavenly Father will also forgive you. 15 But if you do not forgive others their sins, your Father will not forgive your sins" (Matthew 6:14-15 NIV). A lack of forgiveness can keep you in bondage with your past wounds.

We must make sure our past is not terrorizing our future, as Devon Franklin once said. We gotta make sure those open wounds don't dictate our future because we are in bondage from these wounds. This means that you cannot allow your past to dictate every move you make after you've made mistakes, nor can you constantly blame the past. Don't go back to lingering in those things that you don't need to linger in from that open wound. This also mean that you take accountability, you own your mistakes, you own the good you, the bad you, and the ugly you; however, you continue with the consistent intentional efforts of becoming someone new. The new you is not defined by your wounds. The new you doesn't mean you're not you; it just means that you want to live your life a different way and release the old you to become the best you possible. Never let anybody tell you that anything is wrong with shifting your life by becoming the best you that you can be. If someone criticizes you for becoming a better you, they probably don't fit into the group of like-minded people you should keep yourself around. This is that point that I spoke about earlier where you have to start taking inventory of those in your life. It's not to say that you have to cut people off, it means that you just have to have limited contact with some people. As you grow pray for them to grow, and if there comes a time when they come back into your life, pray that they are now healthier people for you mentally. It's awesome for you to give second chances because God always believes in second chances and forgiveness. There are going to be some relationships that simply end since they are terrorizing your future because they are toxic and they are part of what keeps you bonded to those wounds. At times, it is hard to let those things go. Once you realize the things that terrorize your future, check it! Remember: check yourself, before you wreck yourself!

There will be times when somebody says something to you or does something to you that you don't like which always takes you back to that place where you don't want to be. For example, something that has been an open wound for me was my father's addiction and sometimes my mother's lack of emotional support; those are things that over the years always affected me. The good thing is, as I've gotten older I've been able to lessen the blow yet not close the wound fully. I don't feel like the wounds will ever be fully closed, but I've been able to more effectively deal with my open wounds. Even though I feel that these wounds will never fully be closed, I am able to cope with them because I check myself consistently. When I say that my father's addiction is an open wound for me, it means that oftentimes when I see certain things transpire in my father's life, I am taken back to that place when I was a 10 year old girl and he was heavy in addiction and in/out of jail a lot. When I get to that place I must remind myself that all I can do is pray for him and love him as he is. Now I don't want anybody to think that everything is all peaches, roses, and rainbows or everything will just be so great when you visit that old place of the open wound; that is not what I'm saying. You recognize it, check it, and you move on, and then you repeat that process until you feel as free as possible from the bondage of those past wounds. We may have a lot of open wounds but remember it's not an excuse for your irrational or disrespectful behavior. An open wound is a sign that you need to grow past something. This doesn't mean that you will grow overnight, nor does it mean that you'll grow over a year. This may mean that it may take a few years. Rest assured that God will heal you, forgive yourself and others, have faith, pray, be consistent, and be faithful about closing that open wound; your life will eventually get better. Keep in mind, to heal you must deal.

Lastly, we are all different people, and that means we may heal differently. We get over things differently and we work through things in different time frames. What one can get over in two weeks may take another person two years to get over/ heal from. We cannot compare our own time moving past our open wounds to someone else's growth when moving past their open wounds. Bottom line, do not compare yourself to others who are able to move past something at a quicker pace. Comparing will do nothing but keep you living in bondage, tied to those wounds. I've come to the conclusion that some wounds remain open; it's simply a matter of how you choose to cope with them. With consistent and effective coping skills, over time you heal and move forward. With moving forward, you must remember that you will have difficult moments. Ultimately, I do not believe you ever really heal 100% or fully close the wound, you just learn to cope. A great way to release/cope is through writing, sharing, and speaking out to help others while helping you. It's like a double bonus. With that being said, this is why I decided to name my publishing company "Write It Away Publishing," because for me, I was able to cope and work through my issues/past after releasing my first book and spreading my message while helping others. You only get one life, so make the most of it. God doesn't want it any other way.

**(http://www.healthyplace.com/addictions/drug-addiction/causes-of-drug-addiction-what-causes-drug-addiction/#ref)*

A couple great affirmations to repeat to yourself daily in the mirror are:

1. "I effectively deal, forgive, heal, cope, and intentionally press forward. Nothing has the power to hold me back!"

2. "I am creating the BEST me with strong emotional armor!"

3. "I am FREE!"

I want to thank my dear friend and business partner Shaun "Shauny B" Smith for bringing "open wounds" to my attention.

<u>Tanicia "Shamay Speaks" Currie Biography</u>

Tanicia "Shamay Speaks" Currie is a single mother with a full time job, who does not believe in settling in life. Having faced many life challenges, including having three heart surgeries in just 34 years, Tanicia feels that God definitely gave her a purpose. Growing up in a challenging environment with drug addiction in her home, she convinced herself that there had to be more to life than those circumstances. Rather than allow her upbringing to dictate her success, she decided to turn her life's hardships into motivation to persevere in life. She became the first in her immediate family to graduate from college with a Bachelor's degree. In 2009, she went on to open Cause' N A Stir Entertainment, hosting events from concerts to fashion shows to annual toy drives. Tanicia is also the artist relations manager and organizer for the 9quota Awards, which is an annual awards show that honors local arts and talents within her community. Her life changed in 2013 when her daughter Laniyah was born. Laniyah is the best blessing she ever received, but becoming a mother also showed her that it was time to kick life into overdrive. Tanicia is currently the CEO of Branches of Community Services, which helps her give back to those in need. In 2014, she decided to finish the book she started over eight years prior. She published her first book titled "*Deep Within I Knew He Wasn't For Me* in October 2015. Tanicia is a featured author in two empowerment books: *Igniting The Vision* and *Stand Up Be Heard*. Tanicia is currently working with over 10 amazing women, assisting them with accomplishing their dream of becoming published authors, these lovely ladies are featured in Tanicia's compilation titled "Broken Into Brilliance," to be released in June 2017. Her next book will be released late 2017. Being passionate about empowering others to rise above their circumstances and take charge of their destiny, Tanicia's mission in life is to chase all that life has to offer, never give up, and stay humble. Tanicia truly hopes to use her life story, books, videos, workshops, events, and speaking to inspire others to follow their dreams despite their circumstances. Tanicia's theme for 2017 is "Purpose, Progress, and Moving Forward!" Tanicia looks forward to leaving an empowering legacy for her daughter, as well as enjoying the extraordinary journey that God has laid out for her!

"Of Love"

By

Danae Braggs

Age 38

Real Estate Agent ~Author ~ Entrepreneur ~ Speaker

and all around Superwoman

Pittsburg, CA Native

Business Cell: 925-481-6058

From the moment we are born we are taught to put titles on pedestals. For instance, we say things like "a mom will always love and support her children" or "he's the pastor, he would never do that." Titles are just that – titles. They aren't who we are, they are a marker or a description of our place in an order. Titles garner us a minimal and default level of respect just because. Mother, Father, Sister, Brother, Cousin, Pastor, Priest, Doctor, Uncle, etc. I often say "I don't put nothing' past nobody. Anybody can and will do anything." Which basically explains what I'm trying to say in a nutshell.

As our relationships grow we invest so much in the respect of a person's title that we often forget to cast a measured investment of respect into the actual person. Respecting that title more than the person it's attached to and their actions cause our emotions to control situations and reactions towards those individuals. Once we separate the person from the title we can respect the two separately based on the respect they've both earned. For example, your mother is your mother and you respect her for bringing you into this world, but if every time you are near each other there's animosity, negativity, and contention, that probably means there is a lack of respect for the "people" you both are. You both respect the mother-child relationship but the chain of respect is broken or non-existent where it applies to you as a person, and that's ok. Once you realize and recognize what's really going on then you're enlightened and able to correct the situation. In these situations, it doesn't take two. You don't need the other person to meet you halfway. Most of the time they wouldn't anyway; it would be like talking to a brick wall. This is a training moment. You are now able to train this person as to how you wish to be respected and interacted with. At this point you give back only the respect that the person shows you they deserve. Some will only deserve the respect of their title, no more, no less. Some people will never come around. When you see those folks you speak, give a handshake and/or hug, and keep it pushing.

When you take the titles off the pedestals, you lessen the opportunities to be hurt or burn bridges. We are all searching for something we feel is missing. This missing thing creates a strong sense of urgency. The lack of it causes us to react and not respond. It forces us to be complacent and afraid of change, to hold onto things we should let go of, including people. We can't be afraid to release people from their current position in our lives. God will always send someone to fill the void of their absence. What He will not do is replace anyone. Everyone that comes and goes in your life is or was there for a reason. It's their choice to be in your life or to what degree they're involved with you. Their actions, reactions, and interactions with you should dictate their place in your life. Believe what you feel.

So back to this missing thing… I wanted to feel a different kind of love so bad that I did the worst thing anyone could do: I made myself available. No chase. No fight. Just readily available for whatever. I was looking for something, searching for an almost euphoric feeling that really does exist. When I looked back I found that this is something I did all my life.

I made myself available. Feeling needed is often mistaken for being loved or being wanted. I unknowingly made myself available to almost everyone around me. Jobs, family, friends, and/or acquaintances. It was an amazing feeling: I was needed! It was a wonderful feeling, or so I thought. After being needed for years and years and years, I started noticing that some would take what they needed but not give back much or anything at all. I started to feel depleted. I began to realize the difference between being needed and being wanted. When someone wants you around, that want *is* the need. Everything about you, all the attributes you bring with you are what will fill that need.

The rush I got from being needed *seemed* to be the missing thing. If that was the case, how could it be making me feel so bad? It seemed that no one cared about "me." Maybe I didn't really either. Perhaps they all got caught up like I did in the illusion that need equals want. They forgot to treat me like a person. My phone would ring and upon answering, a question would be asked of me. Not "Hi, how are you?", but normally

"Are you busy?" and sometimes not even that. Some calls would be like, me: "Hello," them: "How do you spell…?", "Do you know how I can…?", "Do you know where…?", "How can I…?", "Can you do ……. for me?" etc. This was my life, day in and day out. Then one day in early 2012, I said a pained but fateful prayer. I asked God to show me who was for me and who wasn't, and he did just that. Not only had He opened my eyes but my mind was opened as well. I was so not ready for what became evidently clear. I started seeing people for who they really were. Life changing!

Going forward, I progressed into the mindset that it took to demand the respect for my titles and the person that I've grown to be. I started responding to those texts and calls with "I'm doing great! How are you?" or "I'm fine! Thanks for asking!" BEFORE acknowledging or answering what was being asked of me. For the most part, doing that taught people that I'm actually a person with feelings, not a stoic on-demand robot. This helped weed out the people who genuinely forgot that and truly wanted me around from those that were just takers and were around because they needed something from me. Learning how to sort people out helped me with learning how to love my entire self and therefore truly love others. Remember: flowers cannot grow in sewage. Recognizing the layers of people and where each one fit in my life allows me to grow, replenish what is taken from me, thoroughly heal, and find that missing thing that wasn't really missing at all. Truly loving others for who they are and not how they made me feel is what was missing. That feeling was more exhilarating than being needed. Loving who I have become allows me to fully walk in my purpose.

We must learn to let people want us, not just need us. We have to allow them to chase and fight for us. Our initial affection should be given freely, you know, love thy neighbor. Anything higher than a basic level of respect must be earned in reciprocation. No matter what, we are of love.

Danae Braggs Biography

A Pittsburg, CA native, Danae Braggs is an all-around SUPER WOMAN. Becoming a mother at 16, she had every reason to also become a statistic. She never did. She soared above the odds and surpassed a lot of lackluster expectations. Today she is a successful entrepreneur, real estate agent, and author; just to name a few of her many accomplishments. Her philanthropic endeavors almost always promote her beloved city, Pittsburg. She is also the secretary of Branches of Community Services, a local non-profit focused on giving back to our youth and our community. She is also a featured author in *Breaking Through Barriers Volume 1 & 2.* She has been quoted as saying "I'm from here from here..." An advocate for children, housing rights, self-sufficiency and more, Danae shows and proves that she is the epitome of the term SUPER WOMAN.

Making It Through The Fire

By

Anita Davis McAllister

Age 59

Author~ Child Care Teacher~ Speaker ~Praise Dancer
Spoken Word Ministry

www.Aminah195857.wixsite.com/mysite

Email: spokenwordministry4@gmail.com

Pittsburg, CA

Finding out who I am was an awesome eye opener, because I went through life not knowing who I really was. That was until I had a near-death experience and that is when I finally realized who I was and that God wasn't finished with me yet. Let me take you back a couple of years when my near death experience happened. It was early in the evening on April 9, 2014. The day started off normally, just like any other day; I went to work and came home. Since it was a nice day, I decided to prepare dinner for myself and my husband on the grill outside. Everyone who knows me knows that I love to cook outside on the grill. The sun was beginning to set so I wanted to hurry up and get the food cooked. Since I was rushing I didn't light the grill the way that I normally do. I was putting lighter fluid on the charcoal, but I had forgotten that the type of charcoal I bought already had lighter fluid on it. I then proceeded to light the charcoal and it was at that time a slight wind blew the flame. The flame flew straight up and my hair caught on fire. At the time I was wearing an afro so it took me a while before I realized what was happening. I was just standing at the grill watching it; I didn't realize that my hair was on fire until I heard a sizzling noise and felt the heat from the flames on my head. I immediately ran into the kitchen and tried to put my head under the faucet. I was yelling to my husband for help while I was trying to run water on my head. I remember seeing my hair fall into the sink. I kept yelling for my husband to help me but because he was in the back of the house watching TV is took a while for him to hear me calling him. By the time my husband heard me and came to the kitchen my whole head was on fire and the fire had spread to my clothes. My husband had to rip my shirt off; I didn't know that the fire had spread because I was in such a state of panic. After finally putting the fire out we called 911, since the fire station was down the street from my house it only took them four minutes to get to me. I was in so much pain as I was waiting, all I could say was for someone to call my kids to let them know what was going on. When the fire truck arrived they asked the typical questions about how the fire started and stuff like that. But there was no fire for them to see because only my head had caught on fire and we had put it out before we called 911. My husband had also put the fire in the grill out before they arrived. I wanted to cry but I couldn't because I was in so much pain. Due to the severity of the situation I had to be transported by helicopter. The ambulance drove me down the street to the field at the junior high school. The helicopter took me to the burn center in Davis, CA.

What seemed like a long ride actually wasn't, it just seemed really long because of the pain that I was in. During the ride the paramedics were talking to me about my pain and were trying to give me medication for the pain. I had refused the medication twice and they couldn't understand why I wouldn't want to take it. I explained to them that I didn't like taking strong medicine. When we finally arrived at the burn center I was taken down to the emergency room. The entire room smelled like burnt hair. My kids and my husband arrived at the burn center a short time after I arrived. My pastor, his wife and one of the ministers from my church arrived shortly after them. When my friends and family came into the room to visit me they all had worried looks on their faces. But not me; I was smiling and laughing while I talked to them simply because that is who I am. No amount of pain can take away my smile or joy. I kept thinking that God protected me from the enemy. The way the fire started and how it by passed my face and went straight to my hair, the sound that it made was like a roar. Looking back at the incident I started to remember the sounds that I heard during the fire and I remembered what I saw. This really let me know that God was working in my favor, because the fire could have easily burnt my face but it only got the top of my head.

That same night they had to shave the remainder of my hair off; I was going to be bald. After my hair was all shaved off I didn't want to look at myself. My husband stayed the night with me on the first night, and I was in the hospital a total of seven days. On my fourth day in the hospital a social worker came to see me and talk about the services that they could offer me, such as counseling. I know that the social worker was doing her job but it just seemed as if she was trying too hard to offer me services that I told her I didn't want. It seemed as if she thought that I was depressed and kept offering me services. So I turned the conversation around and started to talk about the goodness of God. This made her stop what she was previously saying and she joined me in talking about God and his word. She even wrote a scripture down about going through the fire and water, Isaiah 43:2 (ESV): "When you pass through the waters, I will be with you; and through the rivers, they shall not overwhelm you; when you walk through fire you shall not be burned and the flame shall not consume you." After the social worker left I never saw her again. On the 5th day I decided to take a walk down the hall in the burn unit, and as I was walking I looked inside one of the rooms and I saw a person with their whole face covered. As I was looking I just thought to myself that that could have been me. Now I really knew that I was blessed by God and that he's not through with me yet. After that realization I knew that I had a lot of work to do and that I was a work in progress. On the 6th day of my hospital stay I was moved to another room on a different floor. I was told that I no longer needed to be on that floor and that they needed the room for someone else. I had second degree burns on my head and third degree burns on my hands. By the grace of God I was healing fast and my hair started growing back. By the time I got back home my hair had already grown 2 inches. On the 7th and last day of my hospital stay I was taking a shower and when I was done I finally decided to look at myself in the mirror. When I saw my reflection, I was actually alright with what I saw. When I was finally released from the hospital the doctor told me that I couldn't go outside for a week. Once that week was up I was able to go outside, but I had to stay out of the sun and keep my head covered. Staying in the house for a week was hard because I'm used to going places, and it also meant that I couldn't go to church. But during the time I was in the house my family and friends came by to visit me. My daughter and oldest son's pastor and his wife came by to visit me as well as some of the members from their church, and this made my stay in the house easier. For some people, being confined to their home for a week would make them miserable, but the Lord had started to work on me and I wasn't about to let misery take over. While I was in my one week confinement I was able to spend more time with the Lord, and I was able to spend more time praying and reading God's word. During this time God manifested in me the ability to write, and that is when I started to write down prayers that I had prayed to God. This was the beginning of the prayer book that God had placed in my heart to write. With the time I was spending in prayer I didn't have time to be miserable; I didn't have time to feel sorry for myself or wonder why this had happened to me. I was maturing in the Lord and receiving all that he was instilling in me. When I was finally able to go back to church I was so excited. A lot of the members were happy to see me, and I received a lot of love from them. Even though I healed quickly I still had to continue going to doctor's appointments so the doctor could check up on how my healing process was going. The doctor had to clip the tops of my ears where it was burned a lot. I was given medication to help with the scars and healing. During my healing process my husband took good care of me. With the three year anniversary of the fire approaching, if you look at me now you wouldn't have known that this had happened to me. I now have a full head of hair and minimal scars from where I was burnt. Getting through this situation without being depressed or feeling lost I truly know was only by the grace of God. I couldn't have gotten through it on my own. I have so much love for my God and I know he loves me. I want to end this chapter with my favorite scripture because it truly fits with the situation I went through. Isaiah 54:17 (ESV): "No weapon formed against me shall prosper." I am so thankful for my life.

Anita Davis McAllister's Biography

Anita Davis McAllister is a resident of the Bay Area. She was born in Detroit Michigan, and at the age of 9 she and her mother moved to California. Anita was raised by a single mother who was very strict in the way she raised her. The morals that Anita's mom instilled in her to become the woman that she is today Anita also instilled into her children. Anita has four children and three grandchildren. Anita was also a single parent and family means a lot to her. Her children are a gift from God and she loves them with her whole heart. Anita has been married for 10 years. She has worked in the childcare field for over 20 years and enjoys every minute of it. She also has worked in the healthcare field as an in-home caretaker for over 10 years. Anita feels that God has placed the gift of writing in her, and she is in the process of launching a prayer book in July of 2017. Anita started Spoken Word Ministry in 2014 and the main focus is bringing people to God and saving souls. In January 2017, Anita became an author and is featured in *Breaking Through Barriers Vol 2*. Anita also has a desire to help people. Recently she joined a group called Bridge Watch Angels whose mission is to prevent people from committing suicide at Golden Gate Bridge. She feels that with a spoken word from God she can help someone in distress. Anita also aspires to start a ministry to help the homeless in her community and beyond. Through her books, ministry group, and public speaking, Anita hopes to inspire others to take charge of their lives and follow their dreams.

My Mess
Turned Into
My MESSage

Broken Relationships

By

Briggette Rockett

(BRIG-jet Rah-ket)

Health, Lifestyle & Career Coach

Email: unmaskyourtruth@yahoo.com &

bodyevolutionbe1@gmail.com

www.unmaskyourtruth.com/

Should love hurt? In the dictionary, the meaning of love is an intense feeling of deep affection, a deep romantic or sexual attachment. When you are 13, what does love really mean? Love has many interpretations for a teenager who is trying to love themselves but doesn't really know how. There were a few boys I thought I was in love with, again, thought. I had no clue what love was about, I was really naïve. I thought my period started because a boy hugged me and I was scared to tell my mother for fear of getting in trouble, so yeah, naïve. When I turned 14, I became pregnant and was placed in a group home until the age of 18 because I longed for love and approval. In my 8th grade year in junior high school, I met a boy who became my first. Because I didn't love myself, the trajectory of my life would change forever. I was shy, insecure, and didn't like the way I looked. I didn't love myself. There was an attractive boy from high school that would come to my school and interact with the girls. I don't know why he came to our school, but looking back I realize it was because manipulation is a lot easier with young minds. I can admit his swag was smooth, cool, his big afro was on point and he dressed nice. I admired him from afar and would listen to the girls talk about how fine he was. Yet, wolves love to prey on the weak. The day came when he set his sights on me, me out of all the other girls, he wanted me. I admit, I felt like the winner, but if I had only known that I wasn't a winner and he wasn't my prince charming, but my nightmare. I was so gullible. If he had told me the sky was purple I would have believed him. He had the power of persuasion, and the ability to smooth talk anyone. I used to tell him he would make a shrewd businessman, but he didn't use his powers for good; everything was about manipulation. When I entered into 9th grade, it was a total mess. During this school year, all I did was skip school and it was all about being with him. Almost every day, I would go to his house and he would make me drink his nasty mixtures of alcohol. I would practically throw up trying to drink it, and if I showed signs of doing so or refused, he would threaten me with physical abuse. This was a red flag but when you are looking for love and not really knowing how to receive it or give it, you don't see the signs. Plus, I didn't see the negative aspects of him at that time, just the good, with hopes he would change. Was this love, stupidity, insecurity, or the lack of love for myself, or maybe all of the above? My emotional feelings were my rationale for staying in a five year relationship of physical and emotional abuse along with the confusion over what constitutes abusive behavior. His abuse involved throwing my belongings, being beaten with a hanger and burned with cigarettes, getting black eyes, a busted lip and having sex against my will. Some of his abuse would take place in front of my daughter. I had become extremely scared of this man; he was Ike and I was Tina. At nineteen, the relationship ended in a final altercation that almost took my life. I was at his mom's house washing clothes when he came in drunk. All I could feel was disgust and decided I wanted to break it off, and he asked me to come to his room to talk. An uneasy feeling started coming over me when he began locking the door that had several locks. He then headed toward his dresser, tuned up the music and reached into his drawer. Before I had a chance to unlock the door, he grabbed me, held me down and began cutting off my hair. I was screaming and trying to fight him, but he had me pinned between the bed and dresser. I couldn't move when he began choking me. I was losing my breath when I heard heavy knocks at his door. His sister heard me screaming and called the police. I was saved. The police asked if I wanted to press charges, I was in tears, devastated, in shock and in disbelief. When I looked up at him, he looked straight in my eyes and murmured, "I will kill you!" I then answered, "No, I just want to go home." When that incident occurred, I didn't tell anyone what happened, because I was ashamed. I told family and coworkers that I decided to cut my hair short, and they looked surprised because I had long beautiful hair reduced to a lowboy cut. It was drastic, but the beautician couldn't save my hair and it had to be all cut off. I never went looking for an abusive relationship especially at 14, who does at any age? I never saw my father physically abuse my mother; arguments yes, but no abuse. When you don't have healthy self-love and can't give yourself an emotional appraisal of your own self-worth, you believe abuse is love. I had no self-care because of the hurt I felt inside; the lack of love for myself led me toward a destructive path and into another physically abusive relationship right after leaving him.

My second relationship started immediately. I was 19 and this was someone who I met in my 9th grade year. He was another older boy that was prowling around, who didn't belong at our high school. He was fine, caramel colored, athletic body, chiseled features, smelled good, and dressed nicely. In 9th grade, my best friend seen him in the hall and she asked me to go over and let him know she liked him so I did. Instead, he indicated that he liked me. I told him I was seeing someone already and that was the end of that. On the day I was departing from my abuser sister's house, I received a phone call and it happened to be him from high school. I was shocked because I had not seen or heard from him since that day in the hall at school, 5 years ago. I wondered what made him reach out or even remember me. We never had any additional conversations, and he didn't even hang in the same circle, it was strange. He said that he retrieved my number from my God-brother. I told him I was in the middle of moving with my best girlfriend to Hunter's Point, and he was happy to hear that because that's where he lived. From that point on, he would come to see me every day after I came home from work. This ended up being a problem for my best friend; she said he was annoying and would call several times or come by before I got home looking for me. It became such an issue that she eventually asked me to leave. With nowhere for me and my daughter to go, I moved in with him at his mother's house on the hill in HP. His mother loved me but wasn't crazy about him, yes, her own son. Shortly after moving there, I lost my job, and we got married. No, I wasn't pregnant. The day he asked me to marry him, we were not doing anything special; it was a nice day, so why not? I put on my red and black checkered suit, he had on some banana-colored leather pants with brown loafers, and we walked to 3rd street looking for his brother to drive us down to City Hall. We arrived minutes before closing and boom just like that, I was married. I used a diamond ring I purchased for myself prior to being with him as my wedding ring and he used a ring he had. I was dreading calling my mother so I waited a few days before I went to the pay phone to give her the good and bad news: one, I was married and two, I lost my job. But I guess for her they were both bad news and of course it didn't go over well. As my journey progressed with this man, my whole life spiraled out of control. I never knew anything about drugs outside of weed and Spanish fly that was unknowingly given to me by my abuser at a Commodores concert. I didn't know the signs of someone on drugs or what type of behavior a person displays, but my now husband started acting strange. He began coming and going, lying, stealing from me, stealing my jewelry, and taking money out of my bank account. He also stole from his mother, which led to her throwing him out. And even though she said I could stay, I wanted to be with my husband. This action led us to being homeless and living in shelters. I sent my daughter to stay with my mother because I didn't want her to experience this life, but one night returning to the shelter thinking we were coming back to cook steak on our hotplate, I noticed a box in the middle of the floor of the lobby with someone's belongings in it. I didn't put much thought into it and we went to our room, but the key wouldn't fit. When we went back to the lobby, we were told that because a child wasn't with us, we couldn't stay there any longer; this was a shelter for families and in order to stay I needed my daughter. This was on a Friday evening after 5pm, and there was nothing that could be done until Monday. I had to call my God-brother and stay with him; my husband had to find another place to stay. I ended up having to get my daughter and go back through the process of getting registered at another shelter. I didn't want her to go through this life, but if I didn't get her I/we would be on the streets and now being pregnant, this was my only option. At 21, on my second child, living in a homeless shelter with a husband on drugs, this was a life from hell. I would cry every night. Before my son was born, we were given permanent housing located in the Valencia Gardens housing projects. After giving birth, my husband's drug use became worse, which led to him physically abusing me, but never the kids. This was not the life I dreamed about, this is not what I believed my marriage would be like; however, like the prior relationship, I was attracted to the positive qualities in him and his looks but failed to see the negative attributes. Here I was again with hopes he would change and do better but things became worse. Over the course of our marriage, I was stabbed, burned with an iron, punched in the face, introduced to crack, had money and food stamps stolen and was consistently lied to. One Christmas, he stole some of the kids' gifts from under the tree. I was here again, in another abusive relationship that was on a whole other level of crazy. My innocence, inexperience, and lack of self-love had yet again led me down another destructive path of an abusive relationship. Turning away was hard because I loved him and we gave vows 'til death do us part, which I took seriously. My belief in love was that you made your husband or man happy no matter what, and that a man would be your prince who would come and take you away to love, cherish and take care of you. Right! No matter what my parents went through, they were together. That is what I understood marriage and relationships were about: through thick and thin, you stay. I had no one to turn to that could offer guidance, support, and understanding. I didn't have a close enough relationship with my mother and father to seek direction. I had no friends to talk to or anyone I could trust. I was alone, trying to do the best I knew how, so I did what I felt in my heart and toughed it out. Then that day came when enough was enough. My uncle who was a police officer now had to get involved because there were drug dealers coming to our home, rocking up because my husband said it was cool, but it turned out he owed them money. These were high profile dealers around my kids rocking up and feeding my husband crack. I was done. When my uncle helped get us out of the mess and relocate, the kids and I went to Double Rock but my husband couldn't come. Our 3-year marriage was over. This was not what I envisioned for my life. I wanted to be a model or a high profile 'someone' in the fashion industry; this life was nowhere close. My world I dreamt of growing-up was nothing like what I was experiencing. I was the oldest child of a middle class family; I was spoiled with all the materials things, a little princess to my family and parents' friends who catered to me. So, how did I get this life? My lack of self-love, insecurity, no confidence and not having a strong support system led me to making the wrong choices in men and poor decisions in life. Domestic abuse can never be part of a good relationship when fear, intimidation, and cruelty are present. How can you call that love? Moving on from those relationships was hard because my sense of commitment and not knowing my worth had me holding on to them. When I found the courage to move on in the second relationship it was because I needed to fall in love with myself and my kids. I also had to move on to achieve something better. I had to focus on our future and what I wanted out of life. What were the goals and accomplishments I wanted to achieve? One was to give my kids what I had been given, which was a stable home. I needed to become a strong woman because my children depended on me to keep them safe. What I walked away understanding from these relationships is that love is not always easy going, enchanting and sincere; real love has it sleeves rolled up with filth, grime and sweat dripping down its forehead. True love asks us to do hard things, almost impossible things, like helping a loved one overcome an addiction again and again, caring for a dying parent, embracing a rebellious child or giving birth. Yes, love is painful, but it shouldn't hurt through physical and emotional abuse. Sometimes the hardest choice to make is to love yourself first before giving it away to someone who will not be worthy. That has been a life lesson for me. Over the course of my life I continued to be involved with men who left me with emotional scars and wondering if my wounds would ever heal. Even though I stepped away from men who physically abused me, I still walked into relationships that would stomp on my self-worth with their drug use, lies, infidelities, STDs, and conceiving children with other women. I have been through it all. This is why I don't judge others when they are going through difficult relationships; I try to provide understanding and perspective. If I am brutally honest with myself, most of the bad stuff that has happened to me was due to my allowing it, which I continue to make peace with; however, because I am strong, I have forgiven. Most importantly, I own my part in the situations and because of that, I still want to believe in relationships. What I have learned is that sometimes to really help people and yourself is to be transparent about your struggle. That allows open dialog for establishing trust and gives validation. Knowing that you are not alone offers strength. For me, unmasking my truth is definitely not easy for fear of being judged, but to be authentic about who I am is essential. When you share your truths, even the ugly ones, it transforms some of the most awful, painful moments into a gift. It helps us gain perspective for ourselves and to help by giving a different perspective to others. This helps us to move on. The difficult experiences will then take their place as part of who we are without defining us, but first we have to take ownership of them. Most people who know me now couldn't imagine me letting someone physically and emotionally hurt me because I am seen as strong and determined. Being weak, insecure or a victim are not qualities most would see in me, so that saying, 'what doesn't kill you makes you stronger,' well, my experiences did just that. I was given strength, and I became more compassionate and have more empathy. My power came into bloom when I was ending relationships or owning up to my part in my divorces. Each difficult step provided the muscle in forgiving myself and those who hurt me. People will do to you in life what you allow them, so setting a foundation that is unwavering will hold you accountable for what you will and will not tolerate within your relationships. High regard for yourself allows for higher standards, so know thyself.

Briggette Rockett (BRIG-jet Rah-Ket) Biography

Briggette Rockett (BRIG-jet Rah-Ket) is a mother of three, two boys, one girl, and has a grandson who she loves to pieces. She loves poetry and is a published poet. She loves fashion, photography, and developing creative business ideas. Briggette is spontaneous, adventurous, and loves to travel. Her curiosity about health and fitness is what led to her transforming herself and leading a group of women to lose a total of 22lbs. Briggette has run 5k's and participated in Fight for Air Stair Climb to raise money and awareness for asthma. She volunteers with various organizations and is currently a volunteer Career Coach at the San Francisco Library. She believes in giving back and does it consistently. At age 14 Briggette became a teen mother, causing her whole life to change, and she was sent to live in a group home until the age of 18. All of her dreams were shattered and a storm formed over her life, hitting hard for several years. Pushing through life's obstacles, Briggette graduated from high school as most improved senior and on the honor roll. Despite the many hardships Briggette faced, she tackled her shortcomings head-on, such as being diagnosed with a learning disability in college; but she didn't let that stop her. She enrolled in a program at the San Francisco Library called Project Read for Literacy, and despite her challenges she became the first female in her family to graduate with an AS, BA, and MA degree along with several certifications in various areas such as Health and Personal & Executive Coaching. Briggette sees learning as a lifelong exploration. Currently, she works a full-time job and is working to establish her health and lifestyle coaching practice. Her practice will promote a reinvention roadmap that empowers people to level-up their minds, bodies, spirits and lifestyles so they can live their most authentic life. Briggette's challenges and struggles are what have given her the voice to reach out and tell her story. Her desire is to be a light of inspiration to others, letting people know that through your mess, you are still blessed. Briggette is a walking testimony that through blood, sweat, and tears, achieving your goals is possible. Lastly, she believes that without self-discipline, success is impossible.

"Beauty & The Beast"

By

Christina Aguilar

Age 33

Author ~ Speaker ~ Aspiring Minister

www.Christinaaguilar33.wixsite.com/author

Christinaaguilar33@yahoo.com

My Name is Christina, and I'm currently in leadership class at my church, Praise Chapel Pittsburg, so God has been really dealing with my heart. With my past hurts and pains, there are things I went through in my life that I don't like talking about. Dealing with my past makes me very uncomfortable. But Jesus loves me so much he wants to heal me from it, and I trust God because He knows best; He's my father. And I don't want to be stuck in bondage anymore.

Here are a few scriptures about bondage:

Stand fast therefore in the liberty where with Christ hath made us free, and be not entangled again with the yoke of bondage. (Galatians 5:1KJV)

Being then made free from sin, ye became the servants of righteousness. (Romans 6:18 KJV)

But the Lord hath taken you, and brought you forth out of the iron furnace even out of Egypt,

To be unto Him a people of inheritance as ye are this day. (Deuteronomy 4:20 KJV)

I the Lord have called thee in righteousness, and will hold thine hand, and will keep thee, and give thee for a covenant of the people, for a light of the Gentiles, to open the blind eyes, to bring out the prisoners from the prison, and them that sit in darkness out of prison house. (Isaiah 42:6-7 KJV) He brought them out of darkness and the shadow of death, and breaks their bands in sunder. (Psalm 107:14 KJV)

Wherefore say unto the children of Israel, I am the Lord, and I will bring you out from under the burdens of the Egyptians, and I will rid you out of their bondage, and I will redeem you with a stretched out arm, and with great judgements. (Exodus 6:6 KJV)

For ye have not received the spirit of bondage again to fear, but ye have received the spirit of adoption, whereby we cry, Abba, Father. (Romans8:15 KJV)

The devil wants me to shrink back and not talk about it because he wants me to stay down and defeated; however, I choose to tell my story and be free.

This is the hardest thing I have had to write about. To be honest, I'm wrestling on the inside from the many years that I held in my pain. I never like to deal with my issues, but I know that I'm in Christ. God wants me to give Him everything and to surrender all the junk. Someone once told me to face my past and let it go. So here it goes.

I remember being a young girl and being molested. Those memories come to my mind and it's like a bad movie being played in my head. I don't understand it sometimes, but I know it happened to me. The thought makes me sick to my stomach. I used to ask why didn't anyone protect me? Being hurt and abused started at a very young age for me and eventually carried into my adulthood and relationships.

These are just a few of the situations that are very hard for me to talk about and deal with. Dealing with past hurt since childhood and later addiction caused me to endure a great deal of pain.

There was a time when I was sleeping with a man who had the same meth addiction as me. We didn't have a title to our relationship but I spent five years in sexual sin with him. This would be one of the many times I ignored the Lord when he would nudge my heart and reach out to me, even though this man I was in sin with would proclaim to me that he was the devil. Even though I witnessed many weird things when I was with him, I still came back, over and over. In bondage to the addiction we had in common. After being in bondage for five years, I started to cry out and ask the Lord to close this door. Not too long after that I found out I had contracted an STD from him, and this made it easier to leave him and come back to the Lord. I had hit rock bottom. Being in bondage and addiction can lead to one forgetting who they are and WHOSE (God's children) they are. (My heart was crushed I felt hurt and depressed by situation; however, I was at my rock bottom, or so I thought.)

There was another time a few years ago when I went to a party. I was very intoxicated and blacked out. Next thing I knew I found myself in a car surrounded by three men that I did not know. Each one took turns performing sexual acts with me. As intoxicated and paralyzed as I was I can still remember that very moment. It makes me feel disgusted and even makes me wonder, why me? Why I didn't stop it? But I know it's a lie from the enemy. Bondage and addiction in my life have allowed the devil to prevail. As painful as it was, I now know that whatever the devil meant to harm me, God would later use for his glory. Just like the men who did this to me, I forgive them. If I firmly want to walk with the Lord, I must forgive and allow God to be their ultimate judge. This scripture comes to my heart: "Then, Jesus said, Father forgives them for they do not know what they do." (Luke 23:34 NKJV) They did not know what they were doing. They were demonically led and on drugs, and this helped me to forgive them. I know the only way to heal from this is to forgive and love the ones who hurt me, just like Jesus did. I also know that I choose not to believe this was my fault. We know that God causes all things to work together for good to those who love God to those who are called according to His purpose. (Romans 8:28 NKJV)

God brought me through that dangerous storm, freeing me from bondage and addiction to now becoming an author as well as stepping into ministry. I now have a husband that loves me and He is serving the Lord as well; however, my past hurts hinder my marriage at times. Since I was hurt by so many men, my lack of trust is a problem in my marriage. Unintentionally, I make my husband suffer for what every man did to me. I know he is a good man but the insecurities within me, at times, hinder the trust I should have for him. But I choose to trust in the Lord. I am allowed to see things more clearly by trusting the Lord more and more. Trust in the Lord with all your heart and lean not on your own understanding; in all your ways submit to Him and He will make your path straight. (Proverbs 3:5-6 NKJV)

When I'm afraid I put my trust in you. (Psalms 56:3 NKJV) Jesus has been with me the whole time; He helped me through those hard times. I know deep down He loves me. Everything I have been through wasn't for me, but for women out there to know that God turned my mess INTO a MESSAGE, and He can do the same for you. Know that there's beauty in all of us, but sometimes we must deal with our inner beast (past hurts) to see our true beauty!

Dear Reader, if you have gone through something like this, you are not alone. It was not your fault; what the enemy meant as harm God will use to turn this mess into a message. Not only do you need to forgive the one who hurt you, but also forgive yourself. I pray for freedom over your life. If you haven't shared the hurt that has happened to you, now is the time. Part of healing is speaking to someone about what happened to you or speaking out to help other women start their healing as you have, and not allowing it to have power over you. You are beautiful, valuable, strong and courageous Never put your trust in people; only God can fill the void, He loves us all so much.

Sincerely,

CHRISTINA

Giving up not an option (Acts 20:24)

"You Are Who You Are" by Russell Kelfer

You are who you are for a reason.

You're part of an intricate plan.

You're a precious and perfect unique design,

Called God's special woman or man.

You look like you for a reason.

Our God made no mistakes.

He knit you together within the womb,

You're just what he wanted to make.

The parents you had were the ones he chose,

And no matter how you feel,

They were custom, design with God's plan in mind,

And they bear the Master's seal.

No, that trauma you faced was not easy.

And God wept that it hurt you so;

But it was allowed to shape your heart

So that into His likeness you'd grow.

You are who you are for a reason,

You've been formed by the Master's rod.

You are who you are, beloved,

Because there is a God.

"The only accurate way to understand ourselves is by what God is and by what He does for us." (Romans 12:3 KJV)

Christina Aguilar Biography

Christina Aguilar is a 33 year old mother of three beautiful children. She is married to a loving man. Christina was born and raised in Pittsburg, California. Christina grew up in a single-parent home. Her father was absent from her life as he battled a drug addiction. During her childhood, Christina struggled with feeling alone, especially without having her father present. Feeling alone and unloved while trying to fill her fatherless void led Christina down a path of drug addiction and self-destruction. After years of ups and downs, Christina was invited to a church that would change her life. She gave church a chance and found that the love she was looking for was in Jesus. She gives all thanks to Jesus for mending her broken heart and allowing her to finally move beyond her past by releasing the pain she held inside. She received deliverance from all addictions and strongholds that held her back in life. In January 2017, Christina became a first-time author; she is a featured author in *Breaking Through Barriers Vol 2*. Christina is currently in the process of becoming an ordained minister. Christina also possesses a love for cosmetology, and she hopes to obtain her license in the near feature. Christina aspires to show others that they can overcome their past and have a brighter future. Through her testimony, books, and future speaking engagements, Christina hopes to motivate others to trust and love God. Christina feels so very thankful and gives God all the glory for the wonderful changes in her life.

Obscurity: The Darkness I Knew

By

Chere' Sifflet

Actor of Television/Film/Theatre

Singer/Speaker/Entrepreneur

www.siffdene@yahoo.com

Find me on Facebook & LinkedIn

I grew up in a family of strong women. One of these strong women was my great grandmother, we called her big mama. She was quiet and sweet. I never heard her speak an evil word against anyone, and she never complained. She served her Lord and her family. She was a faithful usher in her church, and she would help mom with us at times. I remember her good cooking, and afterwards sitting on the floor by her feet when she was done in the kitchen. Sometimes before bedtime, she would prepare some snacks to watch television, and I remember her favorites were oven roasted peanuts and Cheetos.

My grandmother was beautiful to me. She was at least six feet tall and wore clothes like a model. Mom had a lot of pictures of her when she was younger, and she would tell me I got my long arms and legs from her. If she came to church with us on Sunday, I was sure to get a piece of candy from that black purse of hers, which made a lot of noise when it closed.

My mother was a woman of faith and perseverance, and she loved to sing in the choir. The scripture says "Train up a child in the way he should go, and when he is grown he will not depart from it." (Pr. 22v6) She told us stories about how when we were young and living in Los Angeles, one time a burglar came through the window. She gathered her babies and prayed to her Heavenly Father. She said that the burglar left through the same window he came in.

She said we moved from that location with little money and a prayer. Well God answered her prayers, and we relocated to a nicer, safer neighborhood. She had a lot of stories about her God and His faithfulness. These are the strong women I was speaking of, strong because of their trust in God.

I didn't grow up with my father, and I don't remember ever meeting him until I was fourteen years old. The only men I saw on a regular basis were from our church. Our pastor was something wonderful: he was both gentle and strong, and he sure did love the Lord. And the other men would be from the choir, ushers and the church family. We pretty much lived in church; if someone were to ask my address I would have given them Greater Ebenezer Missionary Baptist Church.

I thought at times in my adolescence that we were in church too much, but I learned that growing faith in the Lord God was what I needed to bring me through my second trail of life at age thirteen. The first would be growing up without a father, and the second was being molested by my step-father.

I don't know if I was naturally shy as a child growing up, or if it came as a result of the secret I was threatened to keep. I was told we were a burden, my siblings and I, and that it was hard to take care of us because my father wasn't around. I was told after each time he would sexually abuse me that she wouldn't believe me and that she loved him more than me. He concluded with telling me that if I said anything he would beat me when she left.

Well she left as usual, working to take care of me and my siblings, and sometimes she would leave us to go to choir rehearsal. I lived in torment, wondering and wishing she wouldn't leave me there with him. It became too much and I started running away from home.

I first began running to my grandmother's house, which started fights between my mother and her. I was sent to my father's in Tacoma, WA, and that didn't work out well, because I did not know him.

I was sent back to California and put into a foster home. God said He doesn't put more on you than you can bear, but at age fifteen I thought this was too much. The first foster home I was placed in, the daughter had two beds in her room, and there was already a foster girl there. I wasn't there very long before the caregivers' daughter tried to molest me. I ran screaming, "She's trying to rape me!" I was dragged back in and beaten up. I was removed from that foster home and placed in another home.

My first impression of the woman in the second foster home was that she seemed nice, but sitting around her as she was welcoming me to the home for the first time were two men. Already in fear of my life, all I can tell you is that I was wondering how I would escape this home before either one got a chance to touch me. I don't remember if it was one week or two, but I ran away.

I was homeless, that teenage runaway that you hear about, and I suffered at the hands of everyone I trusted. I had to sleep in so many unconventional places: parks, water heater closets in apartment buildings. As I began to grow older, all I thought about was creating the family image I never had when I was younger. I never knew that would cause me so much pain.

As I was walking down Crenshaw Blvd in Los Angeles CA, I thought I saw my step-father's car. My heart was set to cause him harm, because of the tragedy my life took because of him. The Godly foundation that was instilled in me when I was young, that at times I felt was too much, actually allowed me at that very instant to audibly hear the Holy Spirit say, " You have to forgive him." I didn't even question it. I remember learning about forgiveness countless times from the Bible (Matthew 6:12-15), so I forgave him that day.

I was still, nonetheless, in search of something. I hadn't been home for over seven years and didn't know if my step-father and mother were still together. I had a lot of failed relationships, trying to heal my broken heart with affection because of the sins I experienced.

After these significant trials, the following verses are my heart and mind musings regarding my need for relationships:

Is it your fault that I selected you, even when I saw your weaknesses that I knew would hurt me?

Is it your fault that I didn't trust you with my secrets so you wouldn't add to my pain?

Is it your fault that I was so broken that I created a new family and gave myself a new name so you wouldn't think less of me because of my past?

Is it your fault that I lived with so many insecurities, afraid that you would leave me like so many others did?

Is it your fault, that you just wanted to be my guy, and I needed you to be my father, mother, and shrink...my every breath?

Or was it your fault that you saw my brokenness and took advantage of me?

What if we could help each other instead, instead of hurting one another?

What if we could trust each other with our secrets (what's in our hearts)?

I've come to realize that will never happen on my own; therefore Lord I will wait for you!

I was wrong!

I was wrong to ever look for my healing in past relationships.

I was wrong to seek a relationship before my deliverance.

I was wrong to love you in a way that didn't bring honor to the God I said I'd serve.

I was wrong for not waiting on the Lord. The word says HE who finds a wife finds what is good, and receives favor from the Lord. (Pr. 18:22)

Why did I waste so much of my time doing it my way, trying to resist compromise, but it's sneaking all in the equation? My lack of faith caused my rebellion, to do things my way.

And then I gave up, resigned, surrendered to you Lord! You began to pull back the layers that originated from my childhood tragedies.

Lord, you set in motion the healing of my soul and my mind. Until Lord, it was just you and I; that's when I comprehended that the love I was searching for was there all along.

For the first time I understood what love truly looked like.

I could trust you, and you taught me how to forgive those who sinned against me and caused me harm.

You even taught me how to forgive myself for the sins I committed, and how to honor you with my life and my body.

And then you would send me a husband that loves you more than he does me.

You said all things work together for the good of those who love the Lord and are called.

I survived those tragedies the same way I saw those three strong women in my life survive their trials and difficulties through much prayer. I believe now I am a little like Job in the Bible. He suffered many tragedies in his life as well, but he came to himself and knew that there was a God greater than his trials.

It was about eight years before I was restored back to my family. One day, I ran into one of my mother's friends from the church choir. She invited me to stay, but a point came when she said, Chere' you have to go home. Afraid but tired, a little time passed and I went home.

I remember I was so nervous. I rang the doorbell, I heard my mother walking toward the door, and she was on the phone talking to someone. As she peeped out of the window facing the front porch, I heard her shouting to whom she was speaking "Chere' back, and she looks just like she did when she left."

I had never been happier to see my mother's face. Some time had passed, and she told me that she prayed to her Heavenly Father. She asked the Lord that if my step-father had been touching me to move him out her home. She said two or three weeks after she prayed, he left her keys on the counter and she never saw him again.

I am a witness that prayer changes things, Psalm 143.

The Lord is a healer and a restorer!

Chere' Sifflet Biography

Chere' was born and raised in Los Angeles, California. She was raised in a single parent home and grew up in the Baptist church. Chere' began singing in the church choir at an early age, where she learned to appreciate the sound of gospel music. Gospel music would be a foundation of strength and encouragement for her through the years. She would have to draw on that foundation to be able to keep her faith and persevere through her life's most difficult and challenging trials.

Growing up in southern California, she found herself at Venice Beach, looking to promote her talent. Venice Beach was full of artistic opportunities and it's one of the locations Chere' was discovered as a model. She has modeled for New York West in Newport Beach, CA, and Carolina Leonetti LTD in Hollywood. She has modeled in magazines such as Feeling

Fresh with director Janet DuBoise from Good Times, Scope Magazine, Buick car company, and more.

Chere' is a union actor and she continues to pursue work in the television and film industry to encourage others and to glorify God. Chere' believes the calling on her life is to encourage and to motivate women who have suffered abuse, been rejected or exploited, and have lost hope. She aspires to do this through personal contact, motivational speaking, books, music, theatre, and Christian films.

"It's Not A Pretty Picture, But It's My Picture"

By

Janae Reynolds

Author~Mother

janaereynolds123@yahoo.com

For many years I struggled with the fact that I was not good enough. Always thinking that I was incapable of doing almost anything. Being afraid of success, thinking that successful people thought they were "better than." I never wanted to be "better than." I wanted to be successful, but if it meant that I would look down upon my people than it was something I was willing to give up. My struggle is one that I wasn't proud of for many years. But, in recent years, I began to realize how my struggle actually defined who I am and who I am becoming. My godparents are the ones responsible for introducing to me to my Lord and Savior Jesus Christ. It was October 17, 1989, when I got my second birthright (baptized). It was one of the most important days of my life. When I was 12 years old I remember asking my god-mother "Why does God always show me?" She did not understand my question and responded "He shows us everything." That part is true, but that was not what I meant. I really wanted to know why He chose me to show things to. No I'm not a physic and hell no I can't read you and tell you your future. But God does speak to me clearly and provides visions often. Back to when I was 12 years old; at that age I was fatherless. I had never saw or met my father, and he lived in the same town within a 20-minute walking distance from anywhere in the town. Growing up, my mother never mentioned him, not one word, bad or good. I only knew his name. I remember receiving gifts when I was eight years old (a purple coat) and my mother told me they were from my dad. I was so proud! I wore the hell out of that coat. I remember wearing my coat to my grandfather's house. My grandfather was a dark-skinned man with brown eyes, a bald head down the middle and sometimes salt and pepper furry hair on the sides, he stood all of 5'11 and weighed over 200lbs, and he stayed well dressed in khaki pants and a button up shirt at all times. He grew up in the South, and married my grandmother at 19 years old. He had a third-grade education and was driving an automobile at 12 years old. My grandfather is a hero in my eyes. He was a no-nonsense man that took care of two families and spoiled everyone in his family while raising generations of kids. My grandfather would pick the grandkids up every day from school; rather, he walked on nice days or drove. He was always on time and never complained. The one day I wore my purple jacket, he said to me "You don't want no half-a*s father. If he can't do it 100% of the time, then he can't do it at all." I was no longer proud of my coat. As a mother of three kids (two girls, and one boy) with three baby fathers, that is a statement I have said to each of them. I want my children to be proud of their coats, 100% of the time. Growing up was fun; I spent tons of time with my grandparents. My mother worked a lot and spent little time with me, and the time she spent with me involved her sleeping most of the time, and I resented her for that. I was a child that needed attention. I am thinker, I have questions, and growing up I had many. My mother believed that as long as she provided for me she was a great mother, and she is, but I required time and she missed that part. I love mother to death, we all do. But there are things that she missed or failed me as child that I needed. I have forgiven her for all of those things, because I now know she was giving me her best, and she could not give me what she had not received herself. I acted out as a child, consistently in trouble, and had a mouth that was out of this world. But my mother never gave up on me, she would come to the school whenever they called or send my grandfather to pick me up. I was a fighter; my grandfather would say "You ask a person one time to get out of your face. And if they don't get out of your face, you put them out of your face," and I lived by that. I heard the stories of my mom getting bullied, beat up and made fun of growing up, and I wanted no part of that. I wanted to be different from her, so I chose the fighter position. It's funny the positions you choose as an adolescents are the ones you end up spending your entire adulthood trying to defend. I always thought my mom's approach was timid and I didn't respect it. I wanted her to be brawled up and a fighter like myself. My mother grew up motherless and fatherless. Her mother was an alcoholic and her father never really cared, to say the least. She later shared with me that she had been molested, and that incident played a huge part in her growing up and the creation of her low esteem and never having the ability to defend herself. She felt worthless and ashamed of things that were happening to her.

I was the only child for 18 years; my mother gave birth to me at 17 years old, and I attended her graduation. Eighteen years later she had my sister, and I raised my sister as if she was my own. My mom was a single mother doing her thing. I was spoiled by her, my grandfather, and my godparents. I had the world at my fingertips. I never wanted for anything and always had the best by asking for whatever I wanted whenever I wanted. When I was seven years old my cousins came to live with us, and you can only imagine how I felt. I was now sharing my entire life with three other people. I would be jealous and mean-spirited just because I never had to share and things weren't like they used to be. I thought to myself, she barely has time for me, how can she have time for three more kids? My mother's sister had become addicted to crack cocaine, and was in no position to take care of her children. Instead of allowing the kids to go into the system my mother decided she would take care of them. The beginning was rough, a huge change and adjustment for me. As time went on things got better. My cousins lived with us until they were grown. We only moved three times that I can remember growing up: one apartment and two houses. My mother had a good job and she did her best for us all. After my sister was born, things became different around my house. My mother was acting different, staying up late, moving fast and not really showing interest in my sister. My mother had become addicted to meth. I hated my mom. I hated what she had chosen to do.

I did not understand why drugs were the first thing on the list. I hated her for not being strong. I hated her for caring what people thought of her. I hated her for not loving me enough to choose me instead of the drugs. I hated that she left me for dead. I loved her enough to never give up on her and pray for her and to love her more than I loved myself at times. I became pregnant with my first daughter at 18 years old, giving birth when I was 19 years old. God has a funny way of turning things around in your life. When my mother became addicted to drugs and I became pregnant, my mother went and found my father. One day while I was lying down, four months pregnant at the time, someone knocked on the door. I still lived with my mother at the time. I opened the door, and there stood a man, a woman, and a young girl. My heart began to flutter and my hands were sweaty. I knew exactly who the man was. When I opened the door I stood completely silent, and he spoke: "Hi, I'm your daddy. I know I messed up, and I'm sorry." Growing up, I use to rehearse what I would say if I ever saw him. I thought I would be angry and cuss him out for never calling me or making it to my graduations, buying me McDonalds after school, yelling at him for allowing me to grow up feeling inadequate and unloved. Maybe even punch him for making me feel unwanted or jealous of my brothers and sister for having him be a part of their lives. Instead I did nothing, said nothing. I was numb, I had not anticipated that he would show up with an apology. Was I that simple that a man that had never done anything for me could show up 19 years later with an apology and I say nothing? Where was I? What was going on? I said nothing. I said "Hi, okay." In that moment I was happy, I was excited that he was there. He told me "I know I wasn't there for you, and I'm sorry. But I want to be here for my grandbaby." I understood that. I was okay with allowing him to share in his grandchild's life. In that same moment I was introduced to his wife and my younger sister. I was excited to have another sister. She was pretty and 10 years old at the time. Seeing her made the situation so much easier to deal with. God knew that my mother and I's situation was going to take a turn for the worse, and I now see that he had perfectly planned the comeback of my father at a time when my mother would begin to struggle.

When I was 23 years old and a mother of two, my grandfather passed away. I did not attend the funeral. I remember the feeling. I screamed at the top of my lungs, I had never felt that type of pain in my life. My heart ached for days and I was sick to my stomach and couldn't eat for days. I had no clue where my life was heading. I was lost. My entire support system was being destroyed. I had believed that I was an adult and doing adult things, but I was not prepared for life-crushing events. I was struggling with being a mother, on my own in a verbally abusive relationship with my daughter's father. I was lost. A baby girl at 19 with someone I loved and another baby girl at

22 with someone I loved. I was searching for something I was missing. At that time, I did not know what that "something" was. I grew up fatherless, my mother was on drugs, my grandfather passed away and now my godparents were getting a divorce after 25 years of marriage. At 23 years old I was experiencing my first broken experience. What do you do when your coat begins to tear? I had no clue what to do or where to begin. Everything that was normal to me was changing. I was lost. My whole stability had fallen apart. I spent countless nights crying, sometimes driving around and envisioning killing myself, thinking the worst of myself and my situation. The devil had begun his takeover of my mind. He began telling me that I was worthless and I was better off dead, that the things that were happening to me were my fault. I was breaking up with my first daughter's father, as things had become unbearable for the both of us. He was verbally abusive and emotionally unavailable at that time. We were together (lived together) since I was sixteen years old. He was my first love. I loved him because he reminded me of my grandfather. He was no-nonsense and he made me feel safe. I thought he was the most gorgeous creature I had ever seen, and felt honored that he had chosen me. I was not prepared for the abuse. He would get drunk and cuss me out tell me how ugly I was often. Although I knew he loved me, he did not love me correctly. He was motherless and his first love had abandoned him. The things he felt about women were

taken out on me. I cried, he laughed. I can remember going to take a family picture of him, me and our daughter. As we were getting positioned and waiting on the photographer, he started whispering "You ugly bitch." I did not take the picture. My daughter and her father took the picture that day. Every time I see that picture I am reminded of that day. I did not understand verbal abuse. During that time, I was going through so much that I did not have the mindset to leave him. We had told each other that no matter what, we would stay together to raise our daughter together, and we stayed together for eight years. At age 22, I started dating my second baby girl's father. He was married with four kids, but I didn't care. I loved the way he talked to me, the way he never disrespected me. I enjoyed spending time with him; he was totally the opposite of my first daughter's father. He was caring, compassionate and family-oriented. We got involved to have fun, he was going through whatever with his wife at the time and I was in a horrible place in my relationship. He was my breath of fresh air. We dated for a year and created my second daughter. I remember going to my first daughter's father, telling him I was four months pregnant. We tried to get back together before I had her, but things weren't better. I remember going to the abortion clinic with him, thinking that if we got back together, a child by another man would not help. I didn't get the abortion. My second baby girl's father went to jail on drug charges for three years and things went south for us. He was not present at my daughter's birth and missed two birthdays, although we talked and wrote often while he was in jail. He was no help with the battles I was fighting with his wife and family during this entire time. We struggled with raising our daughter he was not present for eight years. I was frustrated and could not understand why he would not help raise our child. We fought constantly, and I could hear my grandfather's voice: "You don't want no half-a*s father. If he can't do it 100% of the time, then he can't do it at all." In that moment, I knew that God's hand was strumming my pain. I knew that my fatherless childhood was not by accident, it was exactly what I had to go through to raise my fatherless child. I was able to relate and comfort my child and answer those hard questions my child asked about her dad. He had prepared me. It took eight years before he and I got our situation right, but I was happy it did not take 19 years for him to come into my daughter's life. Years passed and I was single, broken and alone. I had male friends that I dated here and there but nothing serious. I was trying to figure myself out. My heart was hard and I trusted no man with it. The break up with my first love was hard, and it took me many years to recover. My self-esteem was low, my heart was broken, and I no longer believed in love. I became promiscuous because I cared nothing about myself and did not know my own self value. I was embarrassed that I had two kids, two baby fathers and single. I did not understand how I was in the place

I was in. It felt like God had left me in the world to figure things out for myself. Most people my age that had parents addicted to drugs were changing their lives and their parents were getting off of drugs. Here I was with a mother who had just begun her journey. It was hard; I was responsible for my sister the majority of the time and when things got worse my mother had to come live with me. Those 15 years were the best life lessons of my life. I never gave up on my mother; we fought often but I never let her go to the streets. The hardest thing I ever did was love my mother through her addiction. There were times when I felt I needed to let her go, but I never had the courage to put her on the streets. I knew that if I kept praying for her and kept doing good and raising my kids, God would remove the addiction from my mother. I was right: 15 years of addiction and now eight years clean. I'm blessed to have witnessed her comeback. I thank God for my journey. It is one that has been perfectly planned out for me. Love is something that I have not been able to master and often times leaves me speechless. Sitting now and looking back over my life, I smile and say "My family is not a pretty picture, but it's my picture."

Janae Reynolds Biography

Janae Reynolds is not shy about enduring tough circumstances. Experiencing a rough upbringing and seeing drug addiction and alcoholism within her family made her believe that she would not take any part in that. At the age of eight years old she accepted Jesus Christ as her Lord and Savior, and began her new journey with the Lord. At the age of 12 she began talking and praying with God often and built an unbreakable bond. As a single mother of two teenage daughters and a two year old son, she has made it her life's mission to always win in life and continue the good fight of faith. With a bachelor's degree in Business Management and her awaited 2017 fall start of her MBA, she continues to improve herself. She believes in education and stops at nothing to push herself and others to always strive for the best, no matter the situation.

Broken to Brilliant Through Forgiveness & Healing

"The Greatest Mistake Of My Life"

By

Miranda O'Hare

Author~Writer~Community Activist

Age 25

Pittsburg, Ca

Email: <u>ohare.miranda@yahoo.com</u>

"Love is blind and our love can sometimes be foolish-our heart doesn't always allow us to love the right person. Sometimes we hurt the ones that love us the most and sometimes we love the ones who don't love us at all." (Unknown) Love allows us to see past the ugliness in the world and see the good within someone's heart. You see the good in someone even if they don't see it themselves. I was taught at a young age that everyone in life is going to hurt you, but it's up to you to pick and choose who is worth suffering for. For me, his name was Daniel. I loved everything about this man; his eyes, his lips, the way he talked, the way he walked. It all turned me on. I was willing to change everything about myself in order to be with him. I wanted nothing more in this world than to have the best relationship we could have. My values, my morals, and my standards were no longer the same; I was becoming someone I no longer knew in order to love someone who didn't even love their own self.

Daniel was everything I wanted in a man. He was tall, dark, and handsome with the juiciest lips I've ever seen. He had a greatest sense of humor and always knew how to put a smile on my face. Did I also mention he had two jobs? In today's society, you'll be lucky enough to find a man who isn't rapping or selling drugs let alone having a job. On top of that he didn't have any kids. I honestly thought I hit the jackpot. He didn't have a high school diploma, GED, driver's license or a car but

I still thought he was worth investing my time in. After all, nobody's perfect and everybody has their flaws. Being the woman I knew I was, I would be able to help him acquire that and more. Like they say "be a boss, date a boss, and build an empire." I felt like there was nothing we couldn't do together.

The relationship was going great and moving fast. We had dinner dates almost every other day and always spent time feeding the ducks at the college. We enjoyed each other's company because we didn't have to travel far or spend money in order to have fun. As long as we were with each other we were happy. Within no time, I found out I was two months pregnant. Being that this was our first child together, we were ecstatic to start a family but everything seemed too good to be true. Daniel began to work late hours at work and it was almost impossible to get ahold of him anymore. I no longer received good morning texts, late night kisses, or calls during my breaks. He also began to receive calls throughout the night from all kinds of numbers. I never really thought too much about it because he had two jobs and worked almost 16 hours a day. It could have easily been one of his bosses calling, but I guess that was the gullible naïve side of me. I soon started to find out about all his skeletons in the closet. As they say "everything that glitters isn't gold." I found out about all the cheating, lies, and other baby mamas. I felt like everything I ever worked for was falling apart.

We decided to take some time away from one another in hopes of healing the relationship but we still kept in close contact. Daniel knew I was considering an abortion and he tried his hardest to persuade me to not go through with it, but my mind was already made up. We eventually got back together, but after the abortion things got worse. Daniel and I began to fight more than ever. It almost felt as though he held a grudge against me for having the abortion. Our arguments got worse and our words became harsh. Before I knew it, he would call me every name in the book. Daniel called me bitch so much that it became a second name for me. Daniel also began making fun of me and ridiculing me. It didn't matter if people were around us or not; I think the attention from other people gave him a high. I had gained some weight from the pregnancy and he used that to his advantage. He would call me ugly and say that I was too fat and hideous to be with anybody. He would always say that he was doing me a favor by dating me because nobody would ever want to be with a girl like me. The sad part is, I actually began to believe him. I no longer saw myself as pretty. I even tried wearing my hair in different styles, wearing makeup, and even dressing differently, but nothing I did was ever good enough for him. I wasn't pretty enough and I damn sure wasn't skinny enough to be with him, but for some reason I couldn't walk away and he wouldn't let me go. After his words and insults started to take no effect on me, Daniel began to get more creative. What started off as open slaps soon turned to closed fists, scratches soon led to black eyes, and before I knew it, I was sleeping with the enemy. The beatings started to become so frequent that I sometimes couldn't leave the house because of all the scars and marks that were left behind (and also because I couldn't do makeup even to save my life). I never admitted this to anyone because I always felt so ashamed of myself. I knew my mother would be disappointed in me because this was not the woman my mother had raised. My mother didn't raise a punk and I sure was acting like one.

I no longer knew who I was and felt like I had lost myself trying to find the perfect man that never existed. I had spent so much time trying to fix a broken relationship that I lost everything about me. I no longer knew what my values or morals were anymore. I no longer knew who I was, what I was becoming or what I wanted in life anymore. All the things I said I would never allow a man to do to me I let Daniel do. I even quit school in order to be with this man, which was a huge mistake. I cut off all my friends and family just to be with him. I no longer went out with my loved ones and separated myself from everybody except Daniel. I dedicated all my time to our relationship and made it the best that it could be. Even though I gave our relationship 1000%, something in my gut told me that Daniel wasn't the one for me but I didn't listen. I ignored every red flag that ever emerged in our relationship. I tolerated and rationalized all of Daniel's derogatory behavior. Like Kevin Hart said "never ignore the signs." I subjected myself to a lot of abuse that I didn't need to endure.

We eventually broke up after I miscarried for the second time with his child; I guess my body couldn't handle the physical abuse anymore. After the break up, I didn't even know what to do with myself. Everything that I worked so hard for was now GONE. I tried to go out but I didn't even feel right. I felt as though I was an outcast of society. I tried to go back to school, but for some reason I couldn't get the hang of the classes, and being surrounded by a large group of people made me really uncomfortable. I tried to hang out with my friends more often but it was no luck. Everywhere I went I could feel this dark black cloud hovering over me. It seemed like I would sit there in slow motion while everything else was moving fast. I felt like the world was moving at a faster pace than me.

Getting myself back together was not as easy as I thought it would be. I was drained mentally, physically, and spiritually. I had to get back on track and make me the center of my own universe. I started to focus more on my needs and wants rather than those of others. Once I realized that my opinion was the only one that mattered, it was easy to get back into the hang of things. I went back to church because I knew that if anyone still loved me, it would be God. I was terrified walking into the house of the Lord because I felt like people could see that I wasn't a Christian or Catholic and I felt like they judged me for it. My mother never raised me to be religious so I didn't really attend church when I was little, but a part of me always knew that there was a higher power. The preacher began to talk about forgiving ourselves and others. He said that forgiving someone doesn't excuse their behavior, it just prevents their behavior from demolishing your heart. It was hard to forgive myself for everything that happened in our relationship. I almost hated myself for allowing Daniel to do so much harm to me. I could have easily left the relationship a long time ago but I didn't. I chose to stay in an abusive relationship and deal with his derogatory behavior. I had to take responsibility for my part in the relationship. I couldn't put all the blame on him, because like they say "It takes two to tango." We both messed up and made mistakes in the relationship that ultimately led to its downfall. I needed to realize that the past is the past and I couldn't do anything about it. I couldn't change it and I couldn't forget it; all I could do is accept it and move on. I had to realize what my values and morals were and understand them. I had adapted to a new mindset and no longer looked at the world or people as I once did.

Forgiving Daniel was not as easy as it seemed; it was easier said than done. At first I didn't think I needed to forgive him because he honestly didn't deserve it. After everything that he put me through, I honestly thought he didn't even deserve to be in my presence let alone deserve an explanation from me. It was hard to accept the fact that I had to forgive him because I still had so much pain and hurt built up inside of me. Every time I looked at him or said his name, I could picture all the horrific things that he had done to me. Even though we were no longer together, I still felt all the pain and hurt that I endured in our relationship. It was almost like a movie that would replay over and over again in my head. Then I realized that this was the exact reason why I needed to forgive him. The truth of the matter was, I needed to forgive him for my own well-being. I needed to forgive him for what he had done to me in order to move on with my life. By not forgiving him, I was giving him power over me. My aunt once told me that you cannot resent someone for not being who you want them to be. Truth was, I did resent him because he wasn't the man I first thought he was. I cannot be mad at him for lying because I already knew he was a habitual liar. I cannot be mad at him for cheating on me because I knew he was a cheater. I can only be mad at myself for believing that he would change even though his actions showed me something different. Deep down inside I knew he wouldn't change. I couldn't resent him for being someone he always was. Forgiveness puts a final seal on what happened to you. Of course you will still remember all the things that were done to you, but you will no longer be trapped by it.

Forgiving Daniel was the easy part; forgiving myself was the hard part. They say that you begin to heal when you let go of all your past hurts, forgive those who have wronged you, and learn to forgive yourself for your mistakes. The road to forgiveness is never easy, and it took me a while until I began to heal and forgive. I had to forgive all those who did me wrong and that wasn't easy at all. Gandhi once said "The weak can never forgive. Forgiveness is the attribute of the strong." I had to let go of a lot of hatred and agony that I was holding onto inside me. Once I had relinquished all the pain and hurt, I was ready to face the world again. I was ready to finally move on with my life and start a new chapter for myself. I first started to spend more time with my family and friends. I felt so guilty because I had turned my back on them for Daniel. I honestly didn't think they would ever forgive me but they did. I also gave school another shot and this time I wasn't going to give up. It was a struggle at first, but with the right support and motivation from my friends, I was able to make it through. With them by my side, there was nothing I couldn't do. After a year, I graduated in May of 2015 with 6 associate's degrees. Whoop whoop! I also began to attend church more. I may not have gone to church as much as I should have but my relationship with the Lord was getting better. I made sure I gave thanks to Him no matter what the situation was or where I was. Without Him, I wouldn't have made it out of that toxic relationship. I began to have a different outlook on life. I tried to always find the good in a situation no matter how bad the circumstances were. Being more optimistic allowed me to see the good in the ugly world that we live in. Being as young as I am, I would have never guessed that I would have dealt with a relationship like this one. Even though Daniel put me in one of the most f*cked-up relationships ever, I could never bring myself to hate him. Daniel was the best mistake I could have ever made. Being with him taught me a lot about relationships and also about myself. If I had never met Daniel, I wouldn't be the woman I am now. I learned a lot from that relationship that that I will be able to take into my next relationship. Everything in life is either a blessing or a lesson; it only depends on how you look at it.

Miranda O'Hare Biography

Miranda O'Hare was born and raised in Pittsburg California, and is the youngest of four children. Miranda was raised by a single mother after her father passed away in 2000 in federal prison. Maranda watched her mother struggle as a single parent as she was bounced around from home to home, living with different friends and family. Miranda saw firsthand what violence, abuse and drugs can do to a family. Miranda refused to follow the same habits that her family had laid out for her. She refused to allow her family's past to dictate her future.

In 2000, Miranda was the first of her family to graduate high school and attend college. In May 2015, she graduated from community college with six associate's degrees. After watching her mother struggle for so many years to provide her family with nothing but the best, Miranda took a huge interest in her community and single mothers everywhere. In 2013, Miranda became a board member of a nonprofit organization called Branches of Community Services which supports the community by providing educational support, resources, and opportunities for personal development. Miranda one day wishes to become a registered nurse and work in a children's hospital.

Young, Dumb & Naïve To Proven Lust

By

Lisa Sanders

Author-Mother- Pharmacy Technician- Songwriter

Age 29

Pittsburg, California

www.LisaTheAuthor.com

ItsLisaTheAuthor@gmail.com

Find on Facebook / Instagram / Gmail

It's been said that forgiveness is a trait of your characteristics that you inherit from one another to bring healing to something new. (Anonymous)

I know that I am a tomboy and always has been. In my life I always dreamed of a guy that would come rescue me from any of my troubles like a damsel in distress and run off into the sunset and live happily ever after, but everyone knows that's how fairy tales go!

In 2007, I thought I had met the guy of my dreams; at the time he was fine as wine, and all mine. We could talk for hours and hang out and do anything young adults would do. I had a checklist for my perfect guy: tall, cute eyes, great personality, and a go-getter just like me. Our motto was "money over everything" and plus, he had a job just like me.

Everything was going great with us; he would take me out to dinner, go shopping, anything you can think of what a perfect guy can be. The thing that I had loved most about him was the bond we had with each other. We both grew up without our fathers, and our mothers had taken care of us. We were both raised by single mothers and that was something we had in common, and we felt bonded by this fact. So we had finally made it exclusive and started dating. He introduced me to all his friends, a.k.a. "his crew," on the block he was living on when he moved into his grandparents' house in Vallejo, CA. I was living with my mother at that time. The relationship was going great. I had a bomb job, working commissionaire for a canteen, making money that I thought I would never make as a young adult.

When we both had time off, we were joined at the hip like Bonnie and Clyde. Nobody could tell us anything about being together at all.

We stayed at each other's houses, stayed out all night until the sun came up, knowing we both had work the next day, but we didn't care at all. As long as we both were in love with one another, we felt that nothing was going to stand in our way and we were invincible. Both our families said it was very unhealthy for the both of us to be around each other all the time. Sooner or later, both of us would both become enemies to each other, but we didn't care at all.

I was determined to prove everyone wrong, his family and my family at any cost. I didn't want them to say to me "You know I was right." Then I set out to prove them wrong so they couldn't say anything to me. I was going to have his back, no matter what, even if I knew he was wrong. Before you knew it, things went left. He lost his job, and his grandparents kicked him out of their home because he started to hustle on the streets. Since he couldn't find another job to work at and he needed money, he was down on his luck. *"Forgiveness doesn't excuse their behavior. Forgiveness prevents their behavior from destroying your heart." (#BEYONDORDINARY)* (*http://www.incourage.me/2013/04/beyond-ordinary-forgiveness.html*)

Next thing I knew, I was with a different person and I didn't even know it. His attitude towards the one he loved was starting to change. He started acting out of the ordinary with me. The first thing he did was start calling me names like "nerd" and "square," as if I couldn't hang with him on the street. So, in my mind, he was another person that I had to prove wrong once again; I had to prove that I wasn't a sucker (coward) and that I can hang. He apologized and I forgave him for that, and we moved on, swept it under the rug like I always do for the one I loved. One night, I decided to look for him on the streets to see if he had a place to sleep and food to eat. He didn't that night, so I got him a room to have a decent night's rest and some food in his belly.

I didn't know that he was high off ecstasy and had been drinking a lot that evening. He told me way late that night, and was yelling at me in front of his friends.

His friends commented on the argument, like "don't let that Bxxxh talk to you like that." He then tried to snatch the keys from me. I told him "You are not going to drive my car," and that is when he hit me in the face, and my braces caught my bottom lips. We were both holding the keys, with one hand fighting with the other, until we both fought ourselves out of the car. I punched him in the face.

We were fighting like cats and dogs. His uncle and his sister had to break us up. We had to be separated that night. The next day he apologized, and I forgave him once again. As the days went by, we got into another argument. As things heated up, I told him "Forget this sxxt, I am going home." He replied "Bxxxh, you are not going anywhere." He pulled a gun on me and flattened all my car tires, so then I was stuck. I didn't have any money because I lost my job at that time, and he broke my cell phone so I was stuck. I began to pray to God to get me out of this situation, and He led me to the house of my friend. From there I was able to call my mom and stepdad to pick me up. Before they got there, he had already left with his friends and was nowhere to be found.

My mother and stepdad got my car towed back home. I was distraught and my bottom lip was swollen. I hadn't eaten in days and I almost lost my life that night. But you know that saying, "Hard head make a soft axx" I still wasn't getting it at all. I thought at that time I would let things calm down. I would convince my mother to give me my car keys back so I could go back to where he was staying. Best believe, it worked and I sneaked out of there.

As he and I drove together on the highway, we got into a bad accident and the car got towed. No one was there to give us a ride back and we were very lost that time.

That night we stayed at his friend's house, and his older friend sexually assaulted me while I was asleep. He left me in the house by myself and didn't tell me anything at all. By that time, I had already gotten kicked out of my house with all the lying I did and for wrecking the car. I had burned bridges, especially with my mother.

Next thing I knew, everything was falling apart for me. The car insurance paid for a rental. I was happy but sad at the same time. It was again he and I against the world.

The arguments still continued, and I almost lost my life once again. The person he had a beef with shot at the car while I was driving. I drove so fast, and ran through several red lights until I reached the train tracks for safety. I knew God was with me again. The bullets didn't hit us, except for the front tire on the passenger side. Thankfully, we only had a flat and no one got killed. As an innocent bystander, I could have died. It was rock bottom for me when I lost everyone who was on my side, and I couldn't call on anyone but God to see me through everything.

"Holding a grudge doesn't make you strong; it makes you bitter. Forgiving doesn't make you weak; it sets you free."(davewillis.org)

One of my family members had given me a Greyhound ticket to live with them for a while, in order to get my life back together. (In my mind, I was thinking "Damn, I am addicted to him like a drug. Now, it's time for me to go for rehab.")

So we had broken up at that time. I began to heal myself from everything I went through with him, the domestic violence and sexual assault. I had to forgive everyone but not forget. I had to pray to the Lord to help me forgive. God helped and guided me a lot while I was out of state and in rehab time.

The first thing I did to cope was to work a lot to stay busy, and to focus on myself and the needs that I had in life. I also set standards for myself, so I wouldn't have to go through this again with my future relationships. I had to do everything on my own without any help from the one who helped me the most: my mother. I provided my own clothes, necessities, food, and transportation to where I needed to go. I decided to give everything to God and read the Bible, which had motivated me ("Yet what we suffer now is nothing compared to the glory He will reveal to us later" – Romans 8:18). (bibleverseimages.com)

I finally moved back to California and started working again. I didn't have a car but God had provided me with a job to that I could walk to every day. I did that faithfully because I knew that when I got blessed with another car, I would not take it for granted. Once I started to forgive more, God began blessing me more; but the one person I needed to forgive me in order to heal was my mother. I had never thought I would hurt her so badly and disappoint her to the point where she couldn't look me in the face. She was so disappointed and hurt by my actions while I was with my ex-boyfriend. So I just kept praying about the situation and our relationship.

I remember one night, a special guest speaker had come to the church and told everyone to speak to who or what hurt and confess our sins to God. I had to apologize to my mother and asked for forgiveness for what I had done to her during my time of destruction. I felt like heaven's gate had opened up. My mother forgave me and we both began to heal with one another, and rebuild our relationship back to how it used to be in the past. I learned at the end of the day the only person who will always have my back through any trials and tribulations in life is my mother.

She was always there with the help of God our Father, because forgiveness is a powerful thing that can change your life and bring a positive light. I knew if I never went through these trials, I would have never known what forgiveness can bring to you in the long run.

I learned that love is a very powerful thing. I also learned that sometimes you might need to take off your blinders, so when someone is on the outside looking in and tries to give advice on a situation, take time to listen to them and acknowledge them in the situation or relationship because they are there to help. Remember, always focus on yourself and your needs first before anyone else's. At the end of the day, it will just be you and God who will always be there for you. Pray all the time and know God wouldn't put any more on you that you can bear.

Never let any man make you feel less than you are because you are beautiful and strong.

Lisa Sanders' Biography

Lisa Marie Sanders was born and raised in Pittsburg, CA. Lisa is a loving mother to her daughter Maliyah. Some of Lisa's interests include dance, teaching/coaching dance, and sports. Lisa possesses two trade school certifications as a CNA and a Pharmacy Technician. She is the first one in her family to complete college. Lisa has always considered herself a role model to young girls and she was once a youth leader at her childhood church Liberty Church of God in Christ. She has a background in cheerleading and being a dance coach for young girls. Lisa considers herself a very kind and caring person who helps others. Lisa has always had a desire to write a book in her lifetime. She truly feels her first book will serve as a legacy to teach and motivate women to be strong, have great self-esteem, and to not fall for anything in life while setting high expectations for themselves. Lisa's future goals include becoming a two-time author, a motivational speaker for young women, and an entrepreneur.

"I want to dedicate this book to my mother Della, my daughter Maliyah, my fiancé Timothy (Killahtrackz) George, and my brother Leon for pushing me to my limit to be an inspiration for someone else."

Lisa Sanders

Broken

Into

Wholeness

My Heart is HIS

By

Angela Jackson

Author ~ Mother ~Intercessor~ Motivator

Age 44

Oakley CA

Email: <u>angela.mitchell79@yahoo.com</u>

Facebook Page: The Well of Everlasting Water

*"Keep thy heart with all diligence for out of it
are the issues of life."*

Proverbs 4:23 KJV

My story begins back in 2010 when one night the Lord gave me a vision. In it, I was in a room and seated at a table. With me were three spirits that were huge in stature, full of darkness, and grotesquely evil. They were discussing the details of my life amongst themselves but I could not hear what was being said. Suddenly, I was knocked down to the floor and on one of my hands was an unfamiliar mark that resembled a tattoo of an emblem which looked like a foreign insignia. At the time I didn't know what it meant but I do remember feeling desolate, very afraid and separated from God, and that perhaps it was a warning of something to come. Within moments Jesus appeared in the room and was sitting next to me. Pure blood began to pour over my body from the top of my head all the way down to my feet. I had the sense that it was the redeeming blood of the Lamb. That vision troubled me and I had no idea that it was a prophetic revelation that was related to my destiny; nor was I aware of the journey that I would take to get there.

"But seek ye first the Kingdom of God, and His righteousness; and all these things shall be added unto you."

Matthew 6:33 KJV

At the time of the vision I was living in a nice apartment, had my very first car and was working at a job that I liked. Life seemed to be good until the day came when I lost my apartment and had to move in with my mother. Fortunately, in September of 2011 my best friend relocated to Chicago so I was able to take over her former cottage in the back of a larger house. I was very happy to have my privacy and independence once again. All during this time I had a steady boyfriend, but then I ended that soul tie in order to wholeheartedly pursue my relationship with the Lord. I knew that He had blessed me to obtain a home in order to spend quiet time in prayer, worship and seeking direction for my life. I already knew that I was called and chosen for ministry and it was time for me to remove myself from carnal distractions.

As the enemy's mission is to steal, kill and destroy and to roam the earth seeking whom he can devour, I got distracted when I met a man and gave unbridled attention to him. As it turned out, he was the grandson of my new landlord so he was always in close proximity of where I now lived. We encountered each other frequently and that fueled the fire for a relationship. I was not necessarily attracted to him at first, but he was very nice and helped me finish moving my belongings into the house, hang pictures on the wall and complete any chore that was needed.

As a reminder, that still, small voice in my spirit would caution me to not fall for him: ***"What about Jesus? I thought you were back here to love on the Lord and have a closer relationship with the Father."*** At the time, I considered that I was actually strong in the Lord; after all, I had been saved since the age of 13 years old, loved the Lord and did all of the so-called right things. I prayed, read the Word, fasted, went to Bible study and to church on Sundays.

Consequently, I proceeded with my own agenda. My new love interest and I spent much time in conversation, sharing ideas and the intimate details of our lives. He divulged secrets that had been told to no one. I felt honored and great compassion because of the things he had experienced. I felt that Satan was trying to consume him, yet I was the woman of God who would save him. Out of these interactions a trust was established and a whirlwind affair blossomed.

"For I know the thoughts that I think toward you, saith the Lord, thoughts of peace, and not of evil, to give you an expected end."

Jeremiah 29:11 KJV

My emotions grew deeper to the extent that eight months later I agreed to marry him.

In having the ability of discernment, there was a part of me that knew I had made an impulsive and very wrong decision, but I pushed it to the back of my mind. The Lord had warned me time and time again not go ahead with it. However, I was the happiest woman alive and no one could tell me otherwise. Although this man was 13 years younger and not a Christian, I did not care. All I knew was that I was in love and that he cared for me; at least I thought he did. I would later learn that my new husband could only provide temporary happiness, if that. He would become a great hindrance and interfere with God's plan. As the flesh is weak, I would become blinded and used by the enemy. We both shared the common need for love and had been searching for it in all the wrong places. We thought that we were what each other had been needing all of our lives. As the months passed he withdrew and wanted to spend less time with me while all I wanted was my husband. He was not employed, and when I returned home from work my house would be filled with all manner of people. There would be drinking and a variety of unsavory activities taking place. He provided no quality time for his wife, abandoning me to run the streets with his friends. Overall, the arguing and problems grew and I began to use heavy drugs. The addiction and stresses of my life resulted in the loss of my job. I felt alone, and I was depressed, miserable and angry. The drug use increased to the extent that I lost 50 pounds within a three month period. I was not healthy and was crying out to God, but nothing was happening. I fell deeper and deeper into depression and attempted suicide more than once. As God would have it, my plans to take my own life failed. Nevertheless, I still felt hopeless.

"Be not deceived; God is not mocked: for whatsoever a man soweth, that shall he also reap."

Galatians 6:7 KJV

Fast forward to June of 2015 when for a brief moment I had decided that I could no longer continue living the life that had sorely become my fate. I left our house with my son, but there was nowhere to go. I only knew was that I had to remove myself from a toxic environment and the man that I was unequally yoked with. My husband was also lost in a world of drugs and impervious to the pain he inflicted upon me. He was not capable of caring for his own outcome let alone mine. The pain and degradation of drug use and the shame of my marriage had become so great that my mother and my daughter did not recognize me nor did they comprehend the person that I had become.

Unfortunately, even though I had left the house, due to the strongholds that kept me bound I remained in touch with and continued seeing my husband. Addiction is not limited only to drugs or alcohol. It also manifests itself in the forms of sexual deviancy, emotional deprivation, psychological dependency and a myriad of dysfunctions in an effort to feel secure, desired, loved, wanted and validated. Being under these influences, I was thinking that we could somehow reconcile our marriage. I still wanted him desperately, even though the

Lord had given His answer. Emotionally weak and addicted to the pleasures of the flesh, I remained in pursuit of a human being rather than an eternal God.

By December 31, 2015, all I wanted was to bring in the New Year of 2016 with my husband. When the clock struck midnight we celebrated a new year together, which also meant a brand new beginning. This celebration of life did not last long. The next day he took my rental car at midnight and did not return until 7:00 am. After all that had happened during the marriage, this was the breaking point to my sanity. I literally lost my mind temporarily and for seven hours straight I screamed, cried, suffered panic attacks and revisited the notion and attempt to take my own life. I couldn't breathe and felt as if I was suffocating. The power of addiction, the spirit of witchcraft and mind control had their vices tight upon me. I was already in a desperate situation, but now I had no job and was struggling to make ends meet by any means necessary. I was still doing drugs as a way to cover the pain that had taken ahold of my life.

In vain, I would cry out to the Lord because all I had was pity on myself. When there was no response from heaven I became angry and bitter. I gave up on God and there was no longer any trust in Him. I stopped praying, didn't read my Bible and I abandoned church. I was hopeless, empty, and ready to give up on life. I didn't care about my children, or anything for that matter. The realization that I had given more love to "man" than I did to the Savior that died for me was a hard pill to swallow.

"There hath no temptation taken you but such as is common to man: but God is faithful, who will not suffer you to be tempted above that which ye are able; but will with the temptation make a way to escape, that ye may be able to bear it."

I Corinthians 10:13 KJV

It was now spring 2016 and the beginning of April. All of my money for the month had been spent. My children had to be taken to school and cared for, and there were bills to be paid. I didn't know how I was going to make it and I was still struggling to accept the ruin brought on by my impulsive marriage. One sunny day while smoking a cigarette in the back yard, the Lord spoke by asking, "***Will you trust me? Will you trust me with your life?***" I gave it some thought with great reluctance, but then remembered that God did not stop being Himself and is still the author and finisher of our faith. My simple answer was, "Yes Lord!"

From that moment on the healing began. I stopped smoking cigarettes and marijuana. I quit drugs cold turkey without any ill effects and asked God to forgive my transgressions. I began praying again and seeking His face rather than His hand. Within a short period of time I was blessed with a job. I didn't have a vehicle but by His grace I managed to meet the demands of getting my son to school and myself to work via public transportation. It was very difficult but I kept my mind and heart on Jesus. I did not allow distractions to set in and I soon came to realize that I had given everything to my husband, but left nothing for God.

"Trust in the Lord with all thine heart; and lean not unto thine own understanding. In all thy ways acknowledge Him and he shall direct thy paths."

Proverbs 3:5-6 KJV

The vision that the Lord gave to me in 2010 was a premonition of what was to come. Though I did not take heed, it was the warning of a man who would enter my life and lead me away from Jesus. The three evil spirits were the demons who would manifest and torture me within my marriage through drugs, sex and separation from God. The emblem imprinted on my hand was representative of the false gods and idolatry that he worshipped. Due to my lust of the flesh, I put man on the throne of my heart where God deserved to have dominion. I had to experience all of the hardships brought on by my own hand in order to be broken with a redemptive return to God and also to share a message with you. We deceive ourselves into thinking that we are right with God, but until we are broken, surrender completely then are restored on the potter's wheel, we will never come into the fullness of the relationship with our Creator. The Lord showed me through His word who I am in Christ and the power and authority that I have inherited through Jesus. Now I long for God; my life and destiny are in His hands. He delivered me from the snares of the enemy. I am no longer bound but I am free, and by His stripes I am healed. Jesus can fill the empty voids and with His living water we shall never thirst.

As I close my chapter I would like to leave you with this message: Remember your first love and let no other gods come before Him. Jesus said that He would never leave nor forsake us; even until the end of the world. Seek Him now, when He can be found. Allow Him to fill you with His love, joy, and everlasting peace. Amen, and again I say, Amen!

Selah!

Angela Jackson Biography

Angela Jackson was born in the greater San Francisco Bay Area on March 25, 1973. She was raised in Daly City/ South San Francisco area. At the tender age of 12 years old, Angela was taken from her birth parents and placed into the foster care system due to sexual abuse at the hands of her father. Her mother could not help her due to the emotional dysfunctions she endured within the household. Angela's first experience of being displaced was entering into a group home where she remained until her 18th birthday. At the age of 18, Angela became a single mother to her daughter.

During her years of growing up in the system, Angela did not have any goals or aspirations due to her experience of growing up in a broken home. From her upbringing and lack of a nurturing childhood, she sought love and acceptance in all the wrong places. By the age of 23, Angela gave birth to her son who was diagnosed with a chromosome disorder called "Partial Trisomy 13." Angela became a single mother of two young children, one having a severe disability.

By 2012, Angela had twice attempted marriage unsuccessfully but soon learned that true love must first be found within and empty voids could only be healed by God. Although Angela had been saved since the age of 13, it wasn't until April of 2016 that Angela was given the divine revelation that the Lord and Savior Jesus Christ was her full portion, and the love she craved had always been there for her to accept and receive.

Today, Angela remains single but restored, whole, happy, and full of confidence and self-esteem. She has overcome the many obstacles that once stood in her way. Angela is very proud of her success as well as the success of her two beautiful children, who are both wonderful people inside and out.

It was through Jesus Christ that Angela's life was turned around and her mess has now become the message that will be shared with many. As Romans 8:28 states, "And we know, all things work together for them that love God, to them who are called according to His purpose." (NJV). Angela's goal in life is to spread a message of how great God's everlasting love, forgiveness, and healing truly is. No matter your age, young or old, and no matter the crisis you may be facing, God remains seated on the throne.

The Take Away (Epilogue)

To end this amazing book, I thought it would be awesome to point out some words of wisdom, or messages, featured in each story. There is definitely more than one message in each story. This book features amazing women from different walks of walk with their ages ranging from 25-60. In my experiences, I believe wisdom is a purely internal thing as we learn lessons at all ages, but the wisdom we gain from learned lessons is the beauty added to the message.

~Broken to Brilliant~

"Open Wounds"

By Author Tanicia "Shamay Speaks" Currie

"Yup, we must "check ourselves!" Check our thoughts, feelings, and emotions to move forward day after day because the wounds are still open. You can't correct what you don't realize. You must BE in and STAY in a place of constant intentional growth and shifting of your life and mindset. You must be aware of the times that you slip back into the old you; you must also accept the old you, check the old you, and be accountable for the new you."

"With that being said, please don't allow others' opinions or fear talk you out of getting help. Counselling can help you cope and slowly work through internal issues from your past, and it helps you get to the root of your problem(s). Many of us want to deal with the problem but not the root of the problem. Think of a tree: you can cut down a tree but the root will remain. This is the same for our open wounds: we can medicate and Band-Aid them but most of the time, the wound remains. If the tree's root remains then it can grow back again, just like your wound."

"There will be times and you will have moments where you have to check yourself! Remember that song, "Check yourself before you wreck yourself" by Ice Cube? There is absolutely nothing wrong with checking yourself and telling yourself to get it together! I check myself all the time because I used to not have a lot of healthy self-control. I don't have total control, but I am intentionally and consistently working at it. I don't just work at it on Monday and Wednesday and Fridays, I work at it at all times. This is a never-ending process, but the beauty is the more intentional and consistent you become, the easier it will be. Consistency is KEY!"

"Of Love"

By Author Danae Braggs

"As our relationships grow we invest so much in the respect of a person's title that we often forget to cast a measured investment of respect into the actual person. Respecting that title more than the person it's attached to and their actions cause our emotions to control situations and reactions towards those individuals. "

"Making It Through The Fire"

By Author Anita McAllister

"With the time I was spending in prayer I didn't have time to be miserable; I didn't have time to feel sorry for myself or wonder why this had happened to me. I was maturing in the Lord and receiving all that he was instilling in me."

~My Mess Turned Into My MESSage~

"Broken Relationships"

By Author Briggette Rockett

"I had to focus on our future and what I wanted out of life. What were the goals and accomplishments I wanted to achieve? One was to give my kids what I had been given, which was a stable home. I needed to become a strong woman because my children depended on me to keep them safe. What I walked away understanding from these relationships is that love is not always easy going, enchanting and sincere; real love has it sleeves rolled up with filth, grime and sweat dripping down its forehead. True love asks us to do hard things, almost impossible things, like helping a loved one overcome an addiction again and again, caring for a dying parent, embracing a rebellious child or giving birth. Yes, love is painful, but it shouldn't hurt through physical and emotional abuse. Sometimes the hardest choice to make is to love yourself first before giving it away to someone who will not be worthy. "

"If I am brutally honest with myself, most of the bad stuff that has happened to me was due to my allowing it, which I continue to make peace with; however, because I am strong, I have forgiven. Most importantly, I own my part in the situations and because of that, I still want to believe in relationships. What I have learned is that sometimes to really help people and yourself is to be transparent about your struggle. That allows open dialog for establishing trust and gives validation. Knowing that you are not alone offers strength. For me, unmasking my truth is definitely not easy for fear of being judged, but to be authentic about who I am is essential."

"Beauty And The Beast"

By Author Christina Aguilar

"Everything I have been through wasn't for me, but for women out there to know that God turned my mess INTO a MESSAGE, and He can do the same for you. Know that there's beauty in all of us, but sometimes we must deal with our inner beast (past hurts) to see our true beauty!"

"I pray for freedom over your life. If you haven't shared the hurt that has happened to you, now is the time. Part of healing is speaking to someone about what happened to you or speaking out to help other women start their healing as you have, and not allowing it to have power over you. You are beautiful, valuable, strong and courageous Never put your trust in people; only God can fill the void, He loves us all so much."

"Obscurity, The Darkness I Knew"

By Author Chere' Sifflet

"Lord, you set in motion the healing of my soul and my mind. Until Lord, it was just you and I; that's when I comprehended that the love I was searching for was there all along.

For the first time I understood what love truly looked like.

I could trust you, and you taught me how to forgive those who sinned against me and caused me harm.

You even taught me how to forgive myself for the sins I committed, and how to honor you with my life and my body."

"It's Not A Pretty Picture, But It's My Picture"

By Author Janae Reynolds

"I thank God for my journey. It is one that has been perfectly planned out for me. Love is something that I have not been able to master and it often times leaves me speechless. Sitting now and looking back over my life, I smile and say "My family is not a pretty picture, but it's my picture."

~Broken to Brilliant

Through Forgiveness & Healing~

"The Greatest Mistake Of My Life"

By Author Miranda O'Hare

"Forgiving Daniel was the easy part; forgiving myself was the hard part. They say that you begin to heal when you let go of all your past hurts, forgive those who have wronged you, and learn to forgive yourself for your mistakes. The road to forgiveness is never easy, and it took me a while until I began to heal and forgive. I had to forgive all those who did me wrong and that wasn't easy at all. Gandhi once said "The weak can never forgive. Forgiveness is the attribute of the strong."

"Everything in life is either a blessing or a lesson; it only depends on how you look at it."

"Young, Dumb, & Naive To Proven Lust"

By Author Lisa Sanders

"She was always there with the help of God our Father, because forgiveness is a powerful thing that can change your life and bring a positive light. I knew if I never went through these trials, I would have never known what forgiveness can bring to you in the long run."

"I learned that love is a very powerful thing. I also learned that sometimes you might need to take off your blinders, so when someone is on the outside looking in and tries to give advice on a situation, take time to listen to them and acknowledge them in the situation or relationship because they are there to help. Remember, always focus on yourself and your needs first before anyone else's. At the end of the day, it will just be you and God who will always be there for you. Pray all the time and know God wouldn't put any more on you that you can bear.

Never let any man make you feel less than you are because you are beautiful and strong."

~Broken Into Wholeness~

"My Heart Is HIS"

By Author Angela Jackson

"It was very difficult but I kept my mind and heart on Jesus. I did not allow distractions to set in and I soon came to realize that I had given everything to my husband, but left nothing for God."

"We deceive ourselves into thinking that we are right with God, but until we are broken, surrender completely then are restored on the potter's wheel; we will never come into the fullness of the relationship with our Creator. The Lord showed me through His word who I am in Christ and the power and authority that I have inherited through Jesus. Now I long for God; my life and destiny are in His hands. He delivered me from the snares of the enemy. I am no longer bound but I am free, and by His stripes I am healed. Jesus can fill the empty voids and with His living water we shall never thirst."

Support Your Local Small Businesses:

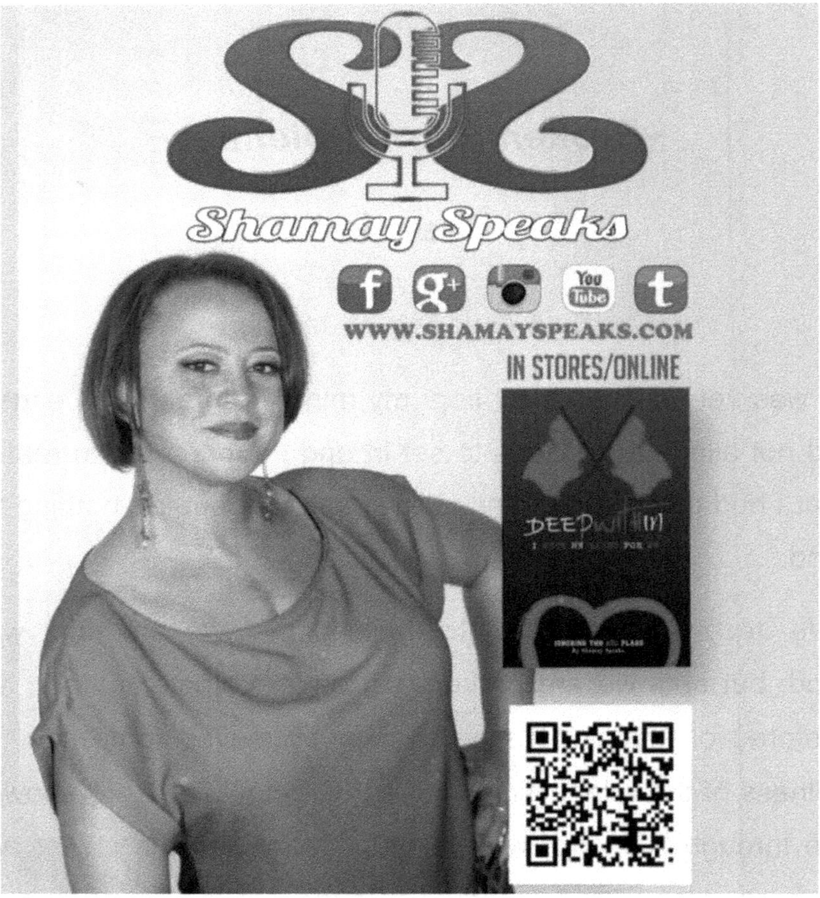

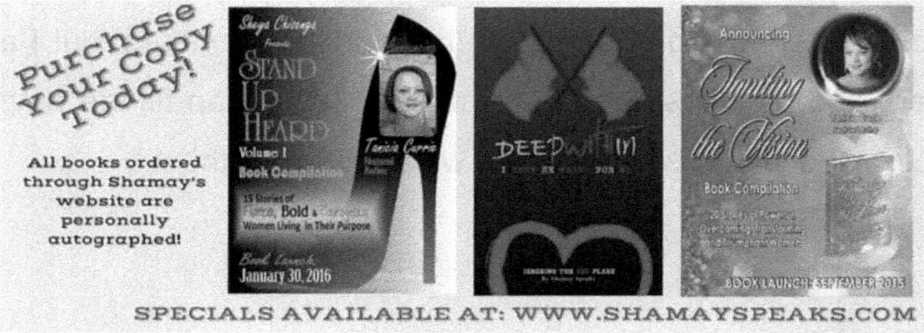

Become a Published Author!!

Let Shamay assist you!

Join Write It Away Publishing's next book compilation, releasing early 2018!

More Information about book compilations and self-publishing workshops, visit:
Www.WriteItAwayPublishing.Com

Contact Shamay with Write It Away Publishing today!

925-421-0221

ShamaySpeaks@gmail.com

Here's what some of the amazing featured authors have to say:

"I would like to thank you from the bottom of my heart, Shamay, for coaching me to become a first time author! Your workshops from start to finish was so informative. You made sure that I had all the resources that I needed to become a author, I would refer any aspiring author's out there to work with you. You were professional, hands on, and very personal. Thank you for also ensuring a safe, fun, loving environment

for me to be successful. Blessings to you. Warm Regards," Andrea McCoy-Taylor

"I am so grateful for the experience to work with Tanicia 'Shamayspeaks' Currie on the Breaking Through Barriers book project. She's such an amazing leader, coach and friend. More importantly, Tanicia always go over and above to make sure her client's needs are met 1000%! Thank you again Tanicia, you've made my first book project experience one of lifetime." Kanishia Wallace

"It was great working with Tanicia. She helped me every step of the way during the process of becoming an author; from compartmentalizing my ideas and getting them on paper to marketing my book and getting my first customer." Rachel Edwards

"Shamay has been a joy to work with. From the first time i met her she was very encouraging and pleasant and very clear on the vision and what she expected of me. She was very professional and is a woman of her word. If she says she is going to do something she does it. She was excellent when it came to meeting deadlines and often met them earlier than promised.

Shamay provided a welcoming atmosphere in all of our workshops and provided great resources and snacks (smile). She made herself available in a way that showed her passion

for not only her vision but our vision and goals. I definitely trust her to publish my next project and will be reaching out to her."

Thank you Shamay! Love, Monique

Since July 2016, Shamay has been the creative visionary and publisher for these amazing and powerful book compilations:

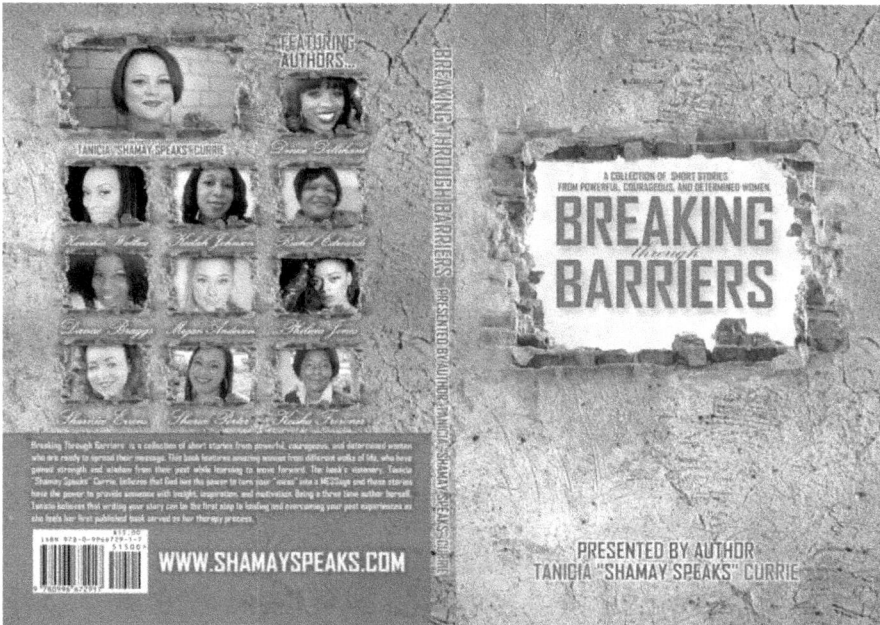

Released July 9th, 2016

July 9th, 2016 I had an extremely blessed weekend. It really had my spirit full. I appreciate all the awesome words the ladies said about me, made me tear up. Everything meant so much to me. My deepest gratitude to every amazing woman who allowed me to assist them in becoming authors.

#BreakingBarriers #Testimonies #Authors #MakeItHappen #SkyisTheLimit #ShamaySpeaks Www.shamayspeaks.com

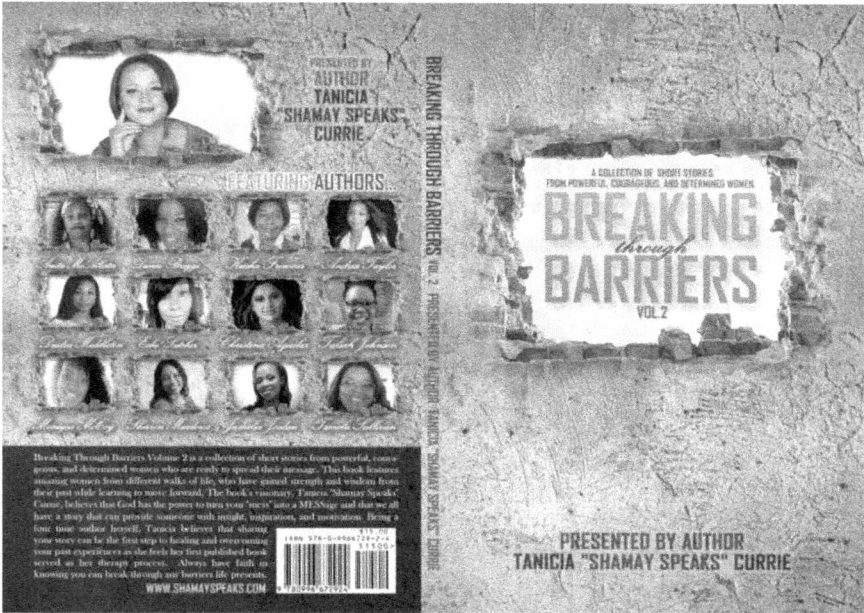

Released January 7th, 2017

January 7th, 2017 I had such a blessed day; words cannot express how I feel. Helping others succeed and be able to bless others. I may provide opportunities but these beautiful women give me the opportunity to assist and guide while walking in purpose. Thank you ladies, for choosing me to work with. It's an honor, congratulations! This is just the beginning♥♥ I'm very proud of each of you continue to step out on faith. Love you y'all! Special thanks to everyone who attended...It humbles me so much the whole experience. It's much more than business, it's about changing lives, providing healing, and stepping out on faith to accomplish goals and dreams. Now I really understand what it means when God said esteem others higher than yourself. Shout out and thanks to my amazing friend and business partner Shauny B Smith for the awesome book cover and my phenomenal cousin for the editing Ilesha Coco Graham and Supreme Photography

Marcus Wright. Beautiful and perfect song by Taliah Johnson and Ben Rivera. #Blessed #Thankful #Grateful #AssistingOtherAmazingPeople I would love to work with more amazing women, if you want to come become an author in 2017 contact me text your email address to 925-421-0221

Live your dreams, anything is possible!

Do you have a book that is finished and you want it published without doing all the research and work to self-publish?

Let Write It Away Publishing help you!

Www.WriteItAwayPublishing.Com

Contact Shamay today for more information and publishing packages!

925-421-0221

ShamaySpeaks@gmail.com

9Quota (925) Art and Music Awards where we give recognition to various artists who contribute greatly to the art, fashion, design and music community. This compilation of talented individuals represent the rich culture of our community and shine light on the up and comers in the area. With the support of the community nominating and voting for these people they get a chance to be inspired as well as inspire others. We have been featured on BET, MTV, Vh1, the Contra Costa Times, East County Times, Mercury News, Oakland Tribune, 89.5 FM Ozcat Radio, and 106.1 KMEL. We are well respected by city officials and always comply with the wishes of the community as well as the Pittsburg Police Department.

This event is completed organized and funded by the 9Quota staff. We take pride in our unique approach in contributing to art in the community. We are fortunate enough to present this event in the historic California Theatre located in the beautiful new revived Downtown Pittsburg area. Previously we have held this event is the Lesher Center for arts in Walnut Creek California and also other locations in Brentwood and Concord. Each winner is presented with a trophy with their named engraved on it to personalize the achievement. We thank all of our supporters.

Branches of Community Services

Tanicia Currie – CEO
Founder- Betty Conner
E-mail: communitybranches925@gmail.com
www.branchesofcommunityservices.org
Business Line: (925) 709-4406
Tax ID #- Available upon request

Our Mission:

Our mission is to support the community by providing branches of educational support, resources, and opportunities for personal development. In fulfilling our mission, we hope to encourage the community to create a cycle of giving back to spread a message of universal community empowerment.

Special thanks to our dedicated team:

Danae Braggs, Shauny B Smith, Miranda O' Hare, Marcus Wright, and all of our supportive and loyal sponsors!

www.KnocksmithMagazine.com

It is no surprise that much of today's media has migrated to online platforms, but there are few truly innovative visionaries who recognize that print, images, videos and music are rapidly converging. One of these leaders is Knocksmith Magazine which is bringing all of these mediums and their fans together to experience something profoundly new and unique.

Knocksmith Magazine offers a physical print magazine that is integrated with online music and video services, via QR apps, codes and giveaways. The production team behind Knocksmith Magazine has showcased some of the emerging superstars of the independent hip-hop scene. The insightful

interviews are presented as videos that are accompanied by written articles and full page images. This rich, interactive media offers a 360 degree view of the artist that can't be found anywhere else in the music industry. In addition to intimate looks at rising musical artists, Knocksmith Magazine is also the platform of choice for fans to explore the music scene. The exhaustive collection of artists and music found on the Knocksmith Magazine catalogue enables fans to hear new songs, link to download sites and find similar artists. Finally, Knocksmith Magazine is a proud supporter of music lovers. Through their "Save the Record Stores" campaign, the magazine is helping to preserve an important but endangered part of the music industry. That is why Knocksmith Magazine encourages purchase of music both online and through neighborhood record stores.

Making a lyrical mar[k]

Producer hopes magazine helps East Contra Costa acts get a footho[ld]

Need an award-winning great designer for book covers and/or graphic design work:

Contact Shauny B Smith with KnockSmith Magazine:

www.KnocksmithMazagine.com

Special thanks to my daughter for being EVERYTHING to me, she changed my life forever. Laniyah you are mommy's BEST blessing. Single mommy life is hard but you give me purpose. I will do everything to show you the way and be the BEST mommy I can be! I love you my HoneyBunn! To all the single mommies out there, I know it's hard to pursue your dreams when you are doing it alone; however, never allow everything to hold you back. Single parents go through many struggles but rests assure that God will see you through. Encourage yourself and don't lose sight of your dream despite your struggles!

Children are a blessing and every person has a purpose from birth,

Laniyah you give mommy purpose!

www.ingramcontent.com/pod-product-compliance
Lightning Source LLC
Chambersburg PA
CBHW071118090426
42736CB00012B/1936